Retrain Your Brain, Reshape Your Body

Retrain Your Brain, Reshape Your Body

THE BREAKTHROUGH
BRAIN-CHANGING WEIGHT-LOSS PLAN

GEORGIA D. ANDRIANOPOULOS, PH.D.

New York   Chicago   San Francisco   Lisbon   London   Madrid   Mexico City
Milan   New Delhi   San Juan   Seoul   Singapore   Sydney   Toronto

Library of Congress Cataloging-in-Publication Data

Andrianopoulos, Georgia D.
   Retrain your brain, reshape your body : the breakthrough brain-changing weight-loss plan / Georgia D. Andrianopoulos.
      p.   cm.
   ISBN 978-0-07-149285-0 (alk. paper)
      1. Weight loss—Psychological aspects—Popular works.   2. Food habits—Psychological aspects— Popular works.   I. Title.

   RM222.2.A523   2007
   613.2′5—dc22   2007026213

BrainMed® Diet and OPT® and versions of such are registered trademarks of Georgia D. Andrianopoulos. Their use herein is strictly limited to this printed publication and the right for the use, publication, or reproduction in any other form, medium, or media, including electronic versions may be granted by written permission only.

1 2 3 4 5 6 7 8 9 0   FGR/FGR   0 9 8 7

ISBN 978-0-07-149285-0
MHID   0-07-149285-2

McGraw-Hill books are available at special quantity discounts to use as premiums and sales promotions, or for use in corporate training programs. For more information, please write to the Director of Special Sales, Professional Publishing, McGraw-Hill, Two Penn Plaza, New York, NY 10121-2298. Or contact your local bookstore.

The nutrition and health information presented in this book is based on an in-depth review of the current scientific literature. It is intended only as a resource guide to help you make informed decisions; it is not meant to replace the advice of a physician or therapist, or to serve as a guide to self-treatment. Always seek competent medical help for any health condition or if there is any question about the appropriateness of a procedure or health recommmendation.

This book is printed on acid-free paper.

For Andria and David

In memory of my father, Demetrios G. Andrianopoulos.
He envisioned and inspired a life of knowledge.

Contents

Acknowledgments

This work would not have been possible without the support of the people who contributed raw material and the editors that helped sculpt and shape that material into this book.

First, I want to acknowledge the people who helped seed the ideas behind this book. My deepest gratitude and affection for my advisor and teacher the late Robert C. Wilcott, Ph.D., for opening up the world of neuroscience for me. I am grateful to Richard L. Nelson M.D. for the decades of tireless support, guidance and for his help reviewing all of my work, including this book. Many thanks to Dan MacDonnell R.N., M.S., for his dedication to the practice of neurofeedback and for his thoughtful feedback that sparked many of the ideas incorporated in to the programs in this book. By far the most enriching contributors to the material have been the people whom I have treated through the years. I would like to thank them for their willingness to share their thoughts and feelings with me. They continue to inspire and motivate me to do better.

Now for the artists, the sculptors of the raw material: I am deeply grateful to my daughter, Andria E. Cress, for using her scientific and literary skills along with her gentle, razor-sharp mind to help edit this book. I owe many thanks to Johanna Bowman at McGraw-Hill for being my unwavering, most empathic "rock" from the very beginning of this project. This book would not have been possible without her diligence, optimism, and dedication. I am also grateful to Dr. Gerald J. Mozdzierz for his gentle guidance and encouragement though this process. Also, many thanks to Susanna Margolis for helping me organize the material.

I want to honor my mother Vassiliki and thank my family, especially my son for the many hours of waiting for me to stop writing. Finally, I want to thank my four sisters, Helen, Konstantina, Anastasia, and Phaedra for carrying the legacy of our parents.

Introduction

If you are going to lose excess weight permanently, if you are going to reshape your body, it's probably best that you forget what you know about overeating and weight gain. I wrote this book to provide a beginning to a new way forward, away from what I perceive as outdated, irrational, ineffective, harmful, and even dehumanizing approaches to weight management.

Don't get me wrong. Weight loss is still a matter of eating less and exercising more, of taking in fewer calories and burning them up more effectively. And the hundreds, if not thousands, of diets out there in all their infinite variety are, for the most part, sound and healthy ways to do just that.

But you can go on diet after diet after diet, as perhaps you have, and chances are you'll continue to gain back any weight you lose. The reason? Dieting attacks only the symptoms of your weight problem, not the cause. To get off the diet weight-loss/weight-regain roller coaster, you'll have to retrain the one organ in your body that really manages eating behavior and weight—your brain.

This book tells you how.

It Really Is All in Your Head

Of course, the fact that the brain regulates our eating is not exactly breaking news. Neurophysiologists have known for more than half a century that the brain controls appetite, and research since then has made it clear that weight gain is a symptom of trouble with the brain's energy regulation systems.

I vividly remember a photograph from my physiology textbook back in my sophomore year of college. Sitting atop a set of laboratory scales were two white, furry animals, one on each tray. I quickly identified the smaller of the two, weighing 520 grams, as a white lab rat. But I wasn't sure about the one on the other scale. It was huge and round, tipping the scale at about 1,080 grams. A strange-looking white cat? Some newly discovered species I hadn't heard about?

The caption told the tale of the two rats: this was a photo of one "normal" and one "hyperphagic" rat. My Greek roots helped me understand the meaning of the word *hyperphagic*: *hyper* = "too much," *phagic* = "food/eating." But being Greek didn't help me understand the mystery—what was causing this rat to eat to the point of weighing more than double the average rat weight? It turns out that the hyperphagic animal ate too much because six months earlier, the area inside its brain that signals satiety (feeling full) had been damaged. Without it, the brain's feeding center had no way of switching off the eating urge, so the rat kept eating pretty much around the clock.

You too have an on/off feeding switch in your brain. It is located in a structure known as the hypothalamus, deep inside the middle of the brain. Ideally, the mechanisms that turn it on and off are balanced between hunger and satiety, allowing you to eat when you're hungry and stop eating when you're full. But I certainly don't have to tell you that it doesn't always work that way! Just about everyone eats for reasons that have nothing to do with hunger. We eat because we are looking for the pleasure that comes from the taste of certain foods. We eat when we are frustrated or bored. We eat for comfort, for escape from fatigue, or when we want to postpone something unpleasant.

In fact, science tells us that thousands of triggers having nothing to do with the basic physiological need for food can turn on the human *eating brain*—the whole network of mechanisms that regulate what we eat, when we eat, and the way we eat.

Once the brain is triggered by all those eating mechanisms, it is virtually unstoppable. So obviously, if you try to counter all this brain power that compels you toward eating by putting yourself on a rigorous regimen of calorie counting or food deprivation, you're pretty much doomed to failure. You may lose some weight—in fact, you probably will—but all you will have done is treat the symptom, not the underlying cause. Unless you do something about the root causes of your desire to overeat, your weight problem will reappear and will probably become a lifelong, nagging pain. We certainly wouldn't think of treating symptoms without looking for root causes in other medical conditions. Think about it: If your child ran a fever for weeks on end, would you be satisfied to continue giving him aspirin and cool baths to lower his temperature? Or would you demand that the doctor do everything possible to determine the cause so you could take action to end your child's discomfort once and for all? Of course, you would do the latter. And that is precisely what you are now going to do about your excess weight—resolve the cause in your brain, not just the symptoms measured on your bathroom scale each morning.

But how?

A Wobble in the Brain

As we've just seen, and as you'll read about in greater detail in the following pages, being overweight is a symptom of a lazy brain or a disruption in the brain's ability to regulate key functions and systems including systems that regulate eating and weight. The scientific term is *global dysregulation,* but the result is the same: lazy brain! Think of it as a little like forgetting to set your watch forward for daylight saving time or back for standard time. Your watch will still work, but your life will be out of sync. In the case of weight management, your brain is managing your weight all right, but it's always a step ahead or behind. Your brain tries to regulate your eating—maintaining balance in all systems is, after all, its main mission—but it falls short. Think of what happens when you arrive late for your first appointment at work on one of your busiest days, when the second appointment is contingent on the outcome of the first and so on. The whole "pyramid" crumbles, and you play catch-up all day. You still manage to carry out most, if not all of the jobs on your list that day, but it's certainly not a comfortable process. Being out of sync makes a huge demand on your energy and can leave you feeling exhausted and frustrated. On top of that, chances are you didn't do as good a job as you could have if you had started your day on time.

This scenario is akin to what happens inside your brain when, for whatever reason, it loses its ability to run smoothly or balance its numerous functions. When the brain is in a state of dysregulation, it behaves similar to you when you're running late: it plays catch-up by robbing Peter to pay Paul. Didn't have enough time to sleep? Have something sweet. You dutifully obey the brain's command and find time to stop for a donut, even when you are running an hour behind schedule. When the brain is not running smoothly, or is *wobbling,* its performance—how well it does its various jobs—also suffers. The brain loses the ability to recognize and maintain a healthy weight. Wobble in the brain consumes resources that might otherwise be used to regulate weight. The parallel is akin to being in the midst of a work-related crisis; issues such as the state of your hair or outfit lose priority! You may also find that you are sleeping poorly, suffer from poor memory, have intense cravings for sweets and carbohydrates, and are often on edge or emotionally raw.

Wobbling also means that the brain's "braking" system, the system that allows you to consider the consequences before eating a whole cake, malfunctions. The result of a lazy brain! So, you proceed to demolish a bag of chips in a matter of minutes, while your better judgment watches in horror.

There's no cause for alarm; this does not mean there is anything "wrong" with your brain or with you. It's just that something has thrown your brain slightly off balance (made it wobble). Eating a cookie can be the brain's way of attempting to regain balance, to run more smoothly and get rid of the wobbling. But, unfortunately, the "balance" it goes back to is also out of kilter.

So how did this dysregulation occur? There is much speculation, but it seems safe to say that along with heredity, your life experiences and personal lifestyle choices had a hand in causing it. Not deliberately and not consciously, but you did it nevertheless. Which means, of course, that you can undo it as well.

How did you cause it? It started back in childhood. (Actually, it may have started in the womb. Your brain could have been programmed to overeat by your mother's nutritional state before you were born.) Her weight and eating habits before and during pregnancy could have altered your food preferences and body weight; increasing your susceptibility to weight gain. However, your eating patterns—how much you eat, the types of foods you desire—continued to be constructed during childhood and throughout your lifetime. The foods you eat today, along with your emotional experiences and physical well-being determine what and how much food you crave tomorrow! Do you ever remember falling and scraping your knee as a kid? Probably your mother or father kissed the wound, then very likely marched you into the kitchen for a cookie, some ice cream, or a piece of cake, which you were assured would make your hurt feel better.

You believed it. Your brain believed it and made sure to remember that trick: pain eases when you eat something sweet. So, in all innocence, a bad eating habit was born—namely, curing pain with food. And not just any food, but heavily sweetened, high-calorie food—the kind that puts on weight in all the wrong places in all the wrong ways. By the way, all sorts of emotional pain, not just scraped knees, can be relieved with sweets.

That's the bad news. The good news is that the brain is a brilliant organ, one that is always learning and always rewiring itself. So what you trained it to do with years of bad or inappropriate eating habits, you can undo by retraining it in another direction.

That's exactly what this book will teach you to do. It will help you retrain your brain to get rid of the wobble—or dysregulation—and prevent you from running toward food as a solution to problems. It will help establish an equilibrium that can make it easier to put on the brakes to avoid consistent overeating. A balanced brain makes you feel best when you are eating healthfully. It sounds simple, and it is.

Follow the program in this book, and you'll learn to rewire your brain. You'll teach it to become better balanced and learn new responses to the wobble, so the next time you get the equivalent of that scraped knee, you'll find comfort and brain balance in something other than a high-calorie sweet treat.

I said it was simple, but I didn't say it was easy. You're up against some stiff challenges—not just the eating patterns you've had for years, but also a food industry and a cultural environment that encourage excessive and inappropriate eating, then hold up extreme skinniness as the ideal of beauty.

But once you understand that the source of your extra weight is a wobble in your brain and that you can straighten that wobble out through conscious effort, you're halfway to your goal of a healthy weight—and to a brain that delivers peak performance in every aspect of your life.

A Fit Brain in a Thin Body—Through Neuroscience

I make this promise of change based on years of research and brain fitness training that have changed the lives of hundreds of patients. My field is physiologic psychology with a focus on eating disorders. I began my work in eating disorders at the University of Illinois College of Medicine, department of surgery, in the mid-1980s; there, I concentrated on studying the role of stress, physical activity, and various diets in gastrointestinal disorders, including cancer. I brought the results of those studies and research to my teaching work in the medical school's departments of surgery and psychiatry and to my job as director of the eating disorders clinic at the University of Illinois Medical Center at Chicago.

Over the years, my own research and the exciting new findings of neuroscience—that is, the study of the brain, spinal cord, and nervous system—became the basis for practical solutions to fight obesity, overweight, and other conditions caused by inappropriate eating.

I was especially encouraged by recent research findings that show we are not doomed to live with the brains we inherited or grew up with. Our brains show neuroplasticity; they are adaptable and can be reprogrammed throughout our lifetime by our daily experiences. They are not "fixed, ended and immutable" as the neuroanatomist Ramón Cajal said in 1913. In 1999, I put it all together in Optimal Performance Training (OPT), the program you'll learn about in this book, and founded Brain Fitness, Inc., a center for the practical application of brain-based tools to achieve weight loss. At our clinics in and around Chicago, the brain is the target organ—front and center—for individuals seeking help with eating and weight regulation. We find that the job of weight management is much easier when the brain cooperates and runs more smoothly.

I've also put this research to work in an eating plan that combines the best of a Mediterranean-style diet (I told you I was Greek!) with the latest neuroscientific findings on foods that promote brain fitness. The BrainMed Diet, as I call it, is also included in this book.

Of course, advances in neuroscience have already given birth to "neuro" solutions to address all sorts of struggles and challenges: depression, attentiveness, and focus, even jealousy. George H. W. Bush's declaration of the nineties as the "decade of the brain" brought this part of our anatomy to the forefront. There are books and lectures and symposia on neurocomputing, neurorehabilitation, neurolinguistics, even neuroacupuncture—not to mention general treatises on how to have a better brain in order to have a better life. Agencies have even entered the field of neuromarketing—using the brain's nature to peddle a specific brand of gym shoe or chocolate cookie.

But in the arena of eating and weight management, it's the food industry that has made the most dramatic use of neuroscientific findings, using what science teaches us about the brain to get to your wallet by way of your stomach.

It isn't just that food manufacturers want you to eat as much as possible; they also want you to eat as often as possible. And they routinely use scientific data to manipulate your brain to get you to do both. They do it in their marketing strategies, and they do it with additives that can actually affect your appetite and your eating habits.

Some of the marketing is pretty obvious. If you watch television, you are bombarded by appealing food commercials aimed at increasing activity in the irrational, emotional, and unconscious part of the brain known as the *limbic system*. That's where the food marketers get you. They don't want you to act rationally at all; they want you simply to react—unconsciously and without thought. So you may be utterly unaware that you're even paying attention to the commercial, yet subliminally that carefully composed TV image of a brownie sundae—or a very attractive person enjoying a brownie sundae—goes right for the emotional part of your brain. Suddenly, almost like one of Pavlov's dogs, you're heading for the fridge or the pantry—or hopping in the car—to do whatever you have to do to obtain that delicious taste.

Some of the marketing strategies are covert. Next time you're in your local supermarket, take a look at the products on the "corners" of the aisles. That's where store managers tend to place the high-calorie snack foods with low nutritional value and high profit margins: chips, cookies, cakes, and the like. The reason? Study after study has demonstrated conclusively that nothing sells as well as corner foods—especially those placed at eye level.

But clever marketing strategies based on years of psychological research are only part of it. Food additives are the other side of the coin, and the food industry is adept at adding components to their food products that manipulate us to crave certain foods and to eat because of cravings when we are not hungry.

It's not that hard to do. As you'll learn in this book, the emerging field of nutrigenomics shows that our brains and even our DNA are actually reconfigured by the foods we eat. Food can turn genes on or off and influence not only your weight and the foods you crave, but health and disease. We've long known, for example, that some people who are exposed to a diet that's high in fats, sugar, and calories early in life tend to become permanently vulnerable to being overweight. And we've learned at least in part why that is so: simply put, those kinds of foods actually stimulate the growth of pathways that connect areas of the brain where addictions are born. Some food ingredients may actually rewire the brain's pathways. This means that your desire for these foods originates in the same brain areas as the desire for addictive substances like heroin or alcohol. Along with the rewiring of the pathways comes behavioral changes—among them, an avoidance of physical activity and an intense desire to taste these comfort foods ("I have to have it now!").

So the food industry has put its laboratories to work to devise manufactured additives and combine nutrients in ways that can have similar effects, producing cravings for specific tastes and specific foods. What's more, they have tried to make these cravings intense beyond anything ever before experienced by the brain, so they are unlikely to be countered by willpower, no matter how formidable. The labs have succeeded admirably, producing foods containing substances that actually manipulate our future eating behavior.

Science is neutral; it's how it is used—and who does the using—that determines its impact. There's nothing illegal about food manufacturers paying psychologists to study human consumer behavior, and it's as fair as anything else in love or war, but this use of science by the food industry has been decidedly one-sided. Until now.

The Optimal Performance Training Program

Optimal Performance Training (OPT) is an exercise program for the brain that concentrates on weight loss, and it works the same way any exercise program works. Think of the skier preparing in autumn for the first snowfall. She'll start with general conditioning to get in good overall shape, then focus on exercises that strengthen her legs and improve her balance and stability. Similarly, OPT exercises are designed to boost the brain's overall performance as well as target specific "muscles" or areas that are especially important to eating and weight regulation.

You'll do this type of training in the three steps of the OPT program:

1. **Discover.** You'll identify and analyze your own personal wobble and see how it affects your eating.
2. **Reframe.** By exploring where your wobble comes from, you'll begin to look at eating in a whole new way. This freshly perceived framework will enable you to focus on what needs changing.
3. **Retrain.** You'll do the "workouts" that will bring your brain to optimal performance so that it seeks equilibrium in healthful living.

The same science the food industry has used to turn your brain into an instrument of weight gain is used in OPT to turn your brain into an instrument of weight loss. You might say we're fighting the enemy with the enemy's own tools, using the same database of neuroscientific findings to help curb overeating and ensure a healthy and manageable weight.

As perhaps the only weight-management program that focuses on brain retraining and rebalancing as the first step to weight loss, the program has seen startling success. OPT graduates don't just lose weight; they gain brain fitness that affects every aspect of their lives, opening those lives to all new possibilities.

That is the kind of success I want to bring to a wider audience. I know that even a few weeks of training can minimize your brain's wobble and set you on the path to a new level of brain fitness and weight loss. Your health and your life will be the winners. After all, no one knows better than you that entanglement with eating is like being chained to food. But the brain that is the first cause of your weight gain is also the thing that can free you from the oppressive burden of being overweight.

Your brain is a remarkable instrument, and it is yours to command. Are you ready to retrain and rewire it away from inappropriate, unhealthy eating—and other wobbles—toward peak performance and permanent weight loss? Let's begin by getting to know this extraordinary weight-loss tool you possess.

PART 1

Discover

Your Brain

An Introduction

Gina had been overweight for as long as she could remember. In her own eyes, her weight defined her, and she
believed it limited her options in life. Like most overweight
Americans, Gina dieted—regularly—to try to get thin. With
each diet, she lost weight, but over time, she put the weight
back on, with a few extra pounds as well. The result was that
Gina found herself engaged in a lifelong struggle, fighting with
herself to gain control of her weight. She could never catch up.
Until she began to follow the program laid out in this book.
First, she identified which part of her brain was causing her to
gain weight. Then she began to retrain her brain away from
the habits that had made her overweight all her life toward new
habits of healthful eating.

Of course, Gina lost the weight she wanted to lose. And
yes, that brought her great contentment and improved her
life in myriad ways. But Gina's own description of this life
change has always seemed particularly instructive, for what
she talks about are not calories, but rather a consciousness:
"I walked down my own street and didn't recognize it. It was
like I had never seen this street before. I noticed the trees and

the houses. I knew they were there before, but I had only perceived them through a different kind of awareness—a lower level of awareness. I realized that I had not really seen my street before."

There's no mistaking Gina's message: changing your life starts with changing your perception, but your perception can only change if you manage to rewire your brain. This is why weight loss is a brain game first and foremost. If you are going to change your body, you must begin by changing your mind—literally. That's exactly what the program in this book will help you do.

Eating on Your Brain

When you order a midnight caramel sundae at the twenty-four-hour McDonald's down the street, it's actually the second time you are ordering it. Your brain ordered it first, and you obeyed by pulling a sweatshirt over your pajamas, jumping in your car, and speeding over to Mickey D's.

> If you are overweight today, the fault is not so much in your snacking as in your cerebrum.

Consider your food hangover the morning after last Thanksgiving. Remember how you felt? A little nauseous, a little dizzy, maybe not too focused: all the vital signs of overindulgence. Yet I'm willing to bet money you did the same thing the previous Thanksgiving, and chances are you'll eat too much again next time.

Why? When it comes to eating, why do we indulge in behaviors that are against our better judgment—behaviors we know will only end in making us feel like guilty failures? True, no one forces us to clean our plates long after we're full or get out of bed and haul ourselves into the night for ice cream, but it's inaccurate to suggest that this is merely a moral failing. The fact is that when it comes to craving eating pleasure, common sense and knowing better go out the window. That's because when it comes to eating, there is something compelling far too many of us to eat inappropriately. That something is the brain.

If you are overweight today, the fault is not so much in your snacking as in your cerebrum—the part of your brain involved in conscious, planned actions such as healthy eating. If your cerebrum takes cues from your stomach more often than from the urgings of your willful common sense, then you will likely find yourself overweight. Looking at the mushrooming rates of obesity in the United States and other Western countries, it certainly looks like more people than ever are listening to their stomachs and the glutton inside their heads than to their reason. Certainly, you are overweight because you eat more than you need to, because you probably eat the kinds of high-calorie foods that put weight on, and because you probably also don't exercise as much as you should. But it's your brain that has been calling the shots on such behavior all this time. It's your brain that determines what you want to eat, how much you eat, and how often you eat.

The food industry has known this for years. It has relied on the very latest in brain research to shape advertising aimed at making you crave specific foods and eat bigger portions. Simply put, the food industry has been messing with your brain, and it has worked. There's no question that this advertising is one reason Americans as a whole have been putting on far too much weight in recent years.

What's going on? How can we blame our brains for our weight gain, for this nationwide near-epidemic of unhealthy, unsightly overweight?

The Brain's Comfort Food

In one way, the answer is simple; in another way, it is terribly complex. What makes it complex is that the brain, which is the heart of the matter, is an amazingly intricate organ that works in very complicated, sophisticated ways, but also in ways that seem simplistic and even silly. I'll have more to say about that later on. For now, the simple answer is this.

The brain is responsible for regulating weight just as it is responsible for regulating all the body's systems and functions. A brain that does this job of weight regulation at peak performance is a stable, well-tuned organ that always strives to maintain a comfortable balance. When something tips the brain off balance, it will automatically try to restore the equilibrium by compensating in some way. For many reasons that have to do with our evolutionary history, the brain's favorite way of compensating is through eating. It conjures up the caramel sundae, and before you know it, you are calling out the order.

The brain chooses eating as its default go-to activity to help rebalance itself for good reasons. The most obvious and deeply coded reason within your DNA is that food delivers instant pleasure. Eating pleasure has a way of quieting down the restless brain, much like it quiets down a restless child—or adult. Its precise purpose is to return your out-of-kilter brain to the balance it finds comfortable. "Feel better," your brain demands, and since satisfying one of your food cravings is a known way to make you happy, your brain in effect will command you to eat, whether your body requires food or not.

This simple prewired tendency to use food as a tool for restoring balance regardless of the type of trouble you are in becomes even stronger with life experiences. Perhaps your parents used food to distract you from a toy you couldn't have or to quiet the tears you shed when rejected by a friend. Specifics aside, it doesn't take much to reinforce eating as a tool for soothing; we come into the world with a brain already programmed to indulge us.

Your brain is not being malicious when it does this. It seeks comfort and satisfaction because these are feelings that keep you in a stable position from which you can succeed. So if you are about to go to bed feeling restless and a little lonely, and you don't feel that you can do anything to solve this problem, the image of the caramel sundae pops into your head. Your brain does a quick evaluation. It sees that you are unhappy, sees how the image of the sundae pleases you, and supposes that eating the sundae may help you feel better. So why not give it to you? Why not throw a little eating pleasure your way to counteract your unpleasant feelings and regain brain balance? Think of it as the brain's way of helping you stay calm and comfortable when you are anything but.

It places the order. You toss on some clothes and drive to McDonald's, where you place the order for the second time. You eat the sundae in the parking lot. It tastes just as you thought it would. It's delicious. It reminds you of childhood. The sweetness lights up your mouth.

But then it's gone, and that's when the problem sets in. The sundae is gone, the delicious feeling is gone, and you're not only back to being restless and lonely, you actually feel worse than ever. Because what is left is a lot of calories you did not need and the knowledge that you have broken the rules. You have violated the number-one weight-loss rule: giving in. You have shown yet again that you suffer from a lack of willpower, and without willpower, you will never lose weight. You are doomed to be fat forever. Unless. . .

What if you could see inside your brain and watch the process that led you to take off like a thief in the night in pursuit of a sundae? Better yet, what if you knew how to have a different reaction to feeling restless and lonely—knew how to see those feelings differently and address them in a different way? Would you still be chasing the sundae? No, emphatically not. A balanced brain leads to a middle-of-the-road, comfortable, fulfilling, and productive lifestyle; it comes up with practical solutions to solve ongoing unmet needs. It doesn't routinely substitute food as a solution to emotional discomfort or routinely push you to extreme cravings that leave you bloated, overweight, and in distress. That's why targeting what's going on in your brain to make you eat the way you do is the one truly effective approach to weight management. It's true, you can't glance inside your brain, see what looks out of place, and readjust it. But you can certainly learn to recognize telltale signs so you can adjust them.

Sometimes your eating brain is triggered by genetic factors or medical conditions that damage your body's ability to regulate weight. However, the majority of overeating is done for emotional reasons—to restore internal balance. Regardless of what's causing your excess weight, a well-balanced brain will bring you closest to what is an achievable, healthy weight for your particular circumstances.

Diets and the Blind Loop

Doctors routinely tell their patients to watch their stress level, start exercising, and stop eating unhealthy food. To be sure, these are all wholesome behaviors that any and all of us would benefit from following, but following them is amazingly difficult when attempted by willpower alone. If you have ever gone on a diet to lose weight, you know precisely what I mean: the force of temptation almost always wins out! The conclusion is simple: dieting cannot be the first step to weight loss; helping the brain flourish must precede the behavioral change of dieting, for it is the brain that regulates our eating behavior. Think of a car that has lost the ability to regulate the way it uses fuel. The driver can see only the obvious problem—that is, that he is stopping at the gas station to refill the tank more and more frequently. The *real* problem, however, is something deep inside the engine itself—a failure in the efficient use of fuel. Is the solution to stop refilling the gas tank? No, it's to intervene at the engine level first, to address the root problem and get the engine back to running as it was designed to do in the factory. Once the engine functions as it was meant to, with all the dynamic efficiency originally built into it, the driver will only need to refill the tank when it is truly empty.

Like most people, you probably think of weight gain in traditional, *linear* terms:

Overindulging = Weight gain

> Dieting cannot be the first step to weight loss; helping the brain flourish must precede the behavioral change of dieting, for it is the brain that regulates our eating behavior.

Seemingly simple and straightforward, this view is nonetheless simplistic at best, leaving little room for exploring other factors that may act alone or in combination to fuel weight gain. Worst of all, as an explanation, this formula is scientifically inaccurate.

All this time, you thought your lack of willpower was preventing you from losing weight. Well, guess what? It's not that simple, and it's not entirely your fault! For years, the message has been that since no one is forcing you to eat, you bear the entire responsibility for cutting back on calories. Since overeating is the cause of your excess weight, the logical conclusion is for you to limit your food intake—to cure your overeating. To execute that task, you're equipped with a doctor issuing dire warnings about the state of your health, a few friends offering encouragement, and a copy of the weight-loss diet of the moment. This linear explanation of weight gain doesn't leave much room for exploring the root causes inside the body—and particularly the brain—that operate behind the scenes to fuel cravings, overeating, and inevitably overweight. Linear explanations lead us directly to linear treatments like diets. Dynamic explanations lead us to treatments of the whole person: feelings, stress, thoughts, and physical health. The OPT program is a dynamic weight-loss program that targets brain fitness to effect healthy eating.

Have you ever walked down the aisle of diet books at a bookstore? Low-carb, no-carb, low-fat, high-fat, rice only, grapefruit, French secrets, the evils of butter, the evils of white sugar, blocks and points—it's enough to send you to the self-help aisle for a book on decision making. If even one of the books is right, then why are all the other ones on the shelf? How can they all claim to offer the secret to losing weight and staying healthy?

In 2006, Americans spent close to $48 billion on weight-loss programs. If dollars spent equaled pounds lost, we'd be a nation of skeletons. Instead, as has been documented time and again, we are heading toward an epidemic of obesity and a host of related conditions and diseases at an alarming rate. Two-thirds of American adults are overweight, and half of those are obese. Clearly, the linear methods of curbing weight gain do not offer a lasting solution.

Another reason for diet failure is the persistent use of *desired outcomes*, like eating less and exercising more, as *methods* for weight loss rather than desired results! But what methods do you use to change your system so you too can adapt these healthy eating behaviors? Certainly, people of healthy weight eat more fiber, avoid high-calorie foods, are active, and manage their stress but that's because their *systems* make it possible for them to eat and live this way. Unless you are given help—methods to rebalance your system so you too can stick to these behaviors—you are set-up to fail.

However, until now weight-loss programs have relied on guidelines "eat less, exercise more, and relax" to be the methods for achieving those same goals. And everyday overweight people dutifully struggle to enact these goals, but since there is a missing link between the tools for achieving the goal and the desired result, they enter a blind loop: they're attempting to reach a goal using only their observations of what that goal appears to be without knowing how to change their behavior.

Time and again, studies have shown that dieting is no match for the physiological forces tugging at your brain. It would be like asking a tugboat to tow the rapidly sinking Titanic to safety—well intentioned, but severely lacking in proper tools.

Every second your brain carries out billions of operations all designed to keep you healthy and thriving. In addition to regulating your emotions and behavior, it is also the key to chemical and hormonal regulation of your metabolism. That means it's biologically sensitive to all internal and external stimuli: your medical condition, a bad night's sleep, an argument with your spouse. The brain receives input in hundreds of forms from thousands of sources and must process it all. So if you're feeling under the weather, have slept poorly, and just quarreled with your spouse, chances are you're going to go off your diet today. Your brain is just getting too much stimulating input; where eating is concerned, its tendency is to roll over.

In fact, time and again, studies have shown that dieting is no match for the physiological forces tugging at your brain. It would be like asking a tugboat to tow the rapidly sinking Titanic to safety—well intentioned, but severely lacking in proper tools. That is no doubt why research consistently shows that most people lose little if any weight on diets, and even more dismally, that 92 percent of those who reach their goal weight will regain it (and then some) within five years.

The evidence is dramatically clear that the appropriate tool for weight loss is not the next diet. No, to lose weight successfully and permanently, overweight individuals need to start with their brains.

Your Most Powerful Weight-Loss Tool: Your Brain

Your brain is an amazing organ. First, I'm going to give you a general idea of the different duties of the different parts of the brain. In Chapter 2, you'll learn some surprising facts about which parts of the brain play a direct role in your eating habits. It's been said that if we were to take our cosmic history of 15 billion years and compress it into one year, human existence relative to that time would be a mere ten hours. But make no mistake. Those ten short hours have been, to say the least, prolific and productive for our species. We have progressed from a mere bundle of potential energy to a central nervous system that has grown in such powerful, complex, and dynamic ways as to boost mere tissue into the glow of consciousness. Thanks to our brains, we are aware of ourselves, and we can imagine, reflect, and think before we eat. At least in theory.

The three-pound wonder, your brain, is made up of roughly 100 billion interconnected cells, or neurons. Neurons "talk" to each other by forming connections or networks. You are capable of forming more than one trillion connections! The more connections, the faster, more creative, and more complex your thinking and the more efficient your actions will be. Arguably, a healthy brain is all you need to thrive in the world, which is why it has been said, "Where there is mind, there is treasure."

You may think of your brain as a single, unified organ, but it isn't. Often, the words *brain* and *mind* are used interchangeably, even though they do not mean the same thing. In fact, most of what we think of as the mind is located in the outer layer of the brain: the cerebral cortex. The remainder of the brain is occupied with basic or vegetative functions and more archaic ways of seeing and interpreting the world around us.

The brain is divided into two halves, or hemispheres: a right and a left. Each half is equally valuable and adds different dimensions that let us know what really is "out there." It is also divided across layers that correspond to different functions: at the bottom we have the hindbrain, also known as the visceral brain; followed by the midbrain, or behavioral brain; and topped with the upper forebrain, also known as the reflective brain. Neuroscientists use these divisions because they best explain behavior, like the caramel sundae excursion.

The older the brain tissue, the lower its location and the more simple its functioning. That's because the first level (visceral brain) was once—millions of years ago—the top honcho, the latest and greatest of what humanity had. A short time later, the environment demanded that we make more and more adaptations to new and pressing needs that faced us. The brain graciously responded. But here's the rub: rather than starting from scratch like tearing down a house, it built new tissue atop the old. When our ancestors' needs changed, the tissue of the midbrain (behavioral brain) was added to handle those needs, and when their needs changed again, the forebrain (reflective brain) was born. The reflective brain houses our big frontal lobes—the reasons we stand on two legs (or the result of standing on two legs), invented the wheel, and have big, bulgy foreheads.

As you can see, the ability of the brain to change and grow according to the demands placed on it by the environment, known as its plasticity, has been around almost as long as humans have. Luckily, your brain retains its plastic (adaptable) quality, so changes in your everyday experiences can result in changes inside your brain.

Let's see if the three layers—visceral, behavioral, and reflective—are good neighbors. How well do they communicate with

Figure 1-1

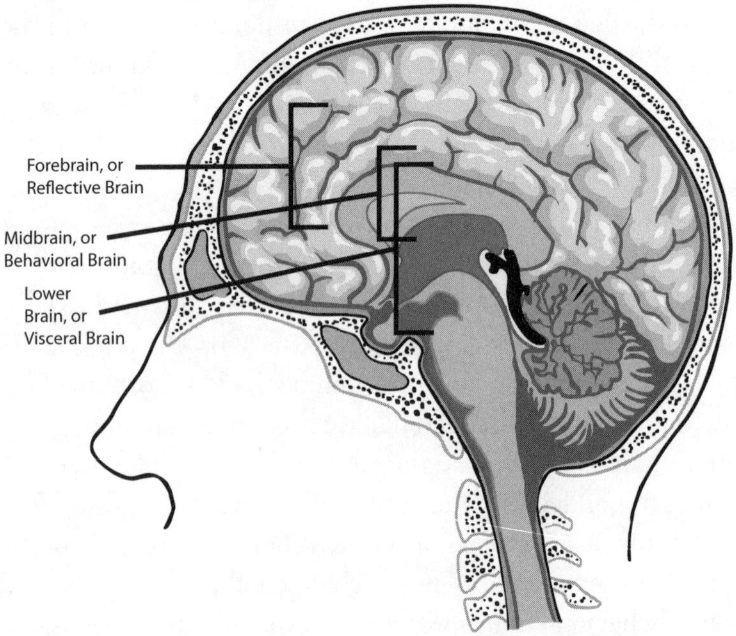

Brain sliced down the middle showing areas that roughly correspond to reflective, behavioral, and visceral components of our actions.

each other? Keep in mind that, like good neighbors, the more connections and free-flowing communication there is between these three levels, the healthier your brain and the more likely the chances that your life is comfortable and balanced.

The Visceral Brain

The visceral brain is totally unconscious. Some of your most clever and devious behaviors lurk here: gut reactions, rage, envy, aggression, and competitiveness. You may want to dismiss such qualities in yourself, but before you do, remember that these core emotional elements have helped us survive over the centuries. The visceral brain is not terribly sophisticated, but it does have street smarts. How else would you spot a liar or have a gut feeling? We can detect danger, hoard supplies, dive into immediate gratification, and lean toward pessimism—all efforts to stay ahead of the game. The visceral brain is the place where our instincts, premonitions, hopes, and that horrible sense of doom originate.

Perhaps even more intense is the fact that this part of the brain provides us with a mental record of to whom and what we are emotionally attached. It keeps track of the foods as well as the people you liked as a kid. You may not be aware of why you have a tender spot for bacon-wrapped hotdogs, but the visceral brain remembers that you ate them on walks with your dad.

The visceral brain is the location of what philosophers and theologians have called "the passions." Neuroscientists place the emotional brain, or limbic system, within it. The main structures that regulate hunger, such as the hypothalamus, and emotional eating, such as the amygdala, caudate nucleus, and hippocampus are part of the primitive component of our actions. They provide us with our prewired likes and dislikes, or *bottom-up* influence over our actions. If you wanted to pin your weight gain on someone else, this might be the place. Freud called it the *id*—a place denoting surging, intense needs that demanded immediate gratification. Here lie the prewired aspects of our behavior: the fear of heights and snakes, the intense pleasure we get from sweet foods and sweet smells.

The lower brain, basically, is Cookie Monster. It is also the point of entry to your stomach as well as your wallet for neuromarketers. The emotional "yum" effect of food is picked up by the visceral brain, and what this part of your brain sees, it wants! Food marketers exploit this part of your nature by rarely providing practical information about the foods they are promoting. They use sensory input to keep you at the visceral level. They know that if they were to present the food images and messages differently—say, simply giving you nutritional facts—you would automatically shift away from the visceral area to the reasoning area of your cerebral cortex. And they know that if you use the reasoning, higher area of your brain, you may take the higher ground and pass on their products.

The Behavioral Brain

Stuck in the middle of the upper and lower brain is the behavioral brain. Like the visceral brain, it is mainly unconscious or automatic, but it can become conscious if needed, which is why we can drive to work without really being aware of each step of the process. The actions we ultimately choose in our daily life originate in the behavioral brain. Philosophers call it the "practical" part of our nature; Freud called it the *ego*. The behavioral brain is caught in a perpetual balancing act: reconciling the blind forces of the visceral brain's demands and the upper brain's high ideals of what we should be doing. The behavioral brain allows for the use of common sense. It is not easily predictable; its talent lies in reconciling forces within the brain and making a decision based on external context. It may feel the pressures from the lower brain to indulge in some sort of passion, but it can hold back long enough to let the upper brain have its say. Because of its location and connections to the upper brain, it can get input about the food in question. Is it too caloric? If so, is there a substitute that will appease the visceral forces? The behavioral brain can reach a middle ground, and you may end up eating low-fat vanilla yogurt instead of ice cream. Not the blasts of ecstasy you had hoped for, perhaps, but the demons are quelled. Until next time.

The Reflective Brain

The final division, and perhaps the most human component of our actions, is the reflective brain. Philosophers and theologians call it the "theoretical," or ideal, portion of our actions. Freud called it the *superego*. As its name implies, this part of our nature allows us to reflect on who we are. We can even reflect on ourselves reflecting! We can tie the past to the present; we attempt to predict and alter the future. It is the supercharged, always-on, fully conscious problem solver, and its entire job is to be your guide and inner advisor.

The reflective brain has connections to the behavioral brain but can perform separately. It needs to be able to disconnect from the behavioral brain in order to consciously analyze decisive action. The reflective brain encompasses the mighty cerebral cortex, the outer layer of the brain, as well as the frontal and prefrontal lobes—the brain's brakes. It is the reflective brain that can delay gratification and postpone any action until all options are explored.

Reflective-brain thinking is also known as *bottom-down* thinking. For instance, when you watch a commercial for food, the reflective brain seizes the information and allots it to various parts of your thinking and memory. It notes the food and compares it to your memories to determine if it is familiar or desirable. It matches the food against your knowledge of calories, carbohydrates, and fat. It considers current weight and diet goals. It does this as fast as your recognition and response occurs, perhaps even faster. You only need a familiar note from a jingle to stir up an entire bout of emotions and possibilities where none existed before.

The reflective part of your brain is responsible for lecturing you. These lectures are nothing more than its attempt to override the behavioral brain. "How will you look if you eat that food? What about your diet? What about your promise? What about that dress?"

This can feel like a true buzz kill at times, but by focusing on facts about the food you are about to eat, you can keep your brain—not your mouth—in charge of your eating choices.

The Balance of Tensions

Why do good people do bad things? Why are our actions sometimes self-defeating? You intend to eat a turkey sandwich, but you end up with a burger, fries, and soft-serve ice cream. If you have often suspected that some of your actions are foreign to you, now you know why. Thanks to your diverse nature, splintered parts of you are pushing in different directions. Behavior is a matter of balancing the three components. Different parts of our brain push in different directions. Whichever segment exerts the most energy wins out. You are the "puppet" that completes their commands.

All three parts of the brain determine our behavior, including eating behavior: desire for food is balanced by nutritional information and awareness of future health and weight goals.

Difficulties with eating, as well as other troublesome areas of our lives, stem from an imbalance in, or tension between, these three components.

Ideally, all the elements of the brain work together to keep the combined energy flow in balance. Maintaining all the brain's systems within a certain energy level relative to one another is essential; unbalanced, they will undoubtedly malfunction. Your head won't spin and your ears won't shoot out sparks, but brain malfunctions can cause rifts that eventually have to be compensated for, like the bugs in a computer system. In fact, in this sense, the brain is really just like a fragmented computer drive; where data is clumped together it will not run as fast as one that has been optimized or defragmented. You defrag your computer to break up lumps of memory into more powerful chunks that are easier to access. Tackling the bugs of your brain will similarly optimize the way you are able to use your brain's energy.

Congratulations! Now you know just enough about the brain to impress your friends. You should also be feeling pretty optimistic. It's not your lack of willpower that's been preventing you from losing weight. No amount of willpower can thwart the brain forces that compel you to overeat . . . at least not consistently. Once your brain has been primed and manipulated by all sorts of things so that your diets were bound to fail.

Now let's find out just what kind of shape your brain is in.

The First Step

Discover Your Eating Brain and Find Your Wobble

The mechanisms responsible for regulating appetite and maintaining normal body weight are located in the brain. Weight gain is a sign that these mechanisms are impaired or out of balance. Since the brain is a dynamic system, an imbalance in a key area like body weight regulation is rarely an isolated symptom; chances are that other areas of the brain are also experiencing turbulence or wobbling. Later in this chapter, you will be given a chance to determine if your own brain is experiencing turbulence by taking the "wobble test."

The Eating Brain

I call it the "eating brain": the set of brain structures and processes, triggers and mechanisms, that regulate our feeding mode—how often we look for food, what foods we find appealing, and how much food we eat. The eating brain has its own design: secret passages, dead ends, deceptive signals, and thankfully, a few helpful road signs. The unique architecture of your own eating brain has developed the way it has due to multiple factors—genetics, environmental pressures, even personal tendencies.

It's impossible to draw a diagram that shows every area and mechanism of the eating brain; there are far too many missing links. However, there are some key components. Several of these eating controls are part of the limbic system located in the midbrain: the hypothalamus, amygdala, insula, and hippocampus. But satiety and eating behaviors are mediated by a host of other networks, including the temporal cortex, cerebellum, cingulate gyrus, and nucleus accumbens.

When these limbic and visceral areas become activated, the desire for food enters the scene—you want something to eat—but in order to actually form a successful plan that will lead to eating, the visceral brain must rely on the reflective brain. Not surprisingly then, the visceral brain has strong connections and relies on the help of structures located above like the frontal lobe and prefrontal cortex, as well as the caudate nucleus and basal ganglia, which are associated with your get-up-and-go, or motor movement.

The locations of the parts of the eating brain are of vital importance because the activity of these locations ultimately determines eating and weight. It means that your eating behavior is the result of the emotional brain (limbic system), your biological energy needs (hypothalamus), and common sense (frontal lobe and prefrontal cortex). In other words, your eating is decided by the work done at the three brain levels we discussed in Chapter 1: the visceral, pleasure-driven part and the reflective, logical part. What you eat and how much depends on the balance of strengths between your "top-down" and "bottom-up" thinking, a job for the behavioral brain. When bottom-up thinking wins, off you go for the caramel sundae, and when top-down thinking prevails, you stay snugly in your seat.

Getting the motor areas of the brain involved in the eating scheme is just a way to get you out of your chair and to the nearest food source.

Numerous brain areas are involved in overeating, but four can readily be identified because they leave their telltale sign on your particular overeating patterns.

The Prefrontal Cortex

As with almost every brain structure, you have two: left and right. The prefrontal cortex is located above your eyebrows and ends roughly above your ears. It forms the tip of the frontal lobe and is part of the reflective brain—the latest and greatest in brain tissue. The prefrontal cortex helps you postpone gratification. A mighty prefrontal cortex is a must for passing on seconds or walking away from the dessert table. Think of it as the brain's equivalent of a brake system. The human ability to postpone gratification or inhibit something you desire rests primarily with the frontal lobe and prefrontal cortex. If, for whatever reason, this area is underactive, the brain's brakes are sluggish. You may end up acting impulsively and engage in many self-defeating behaviors, or lazy brain behaviors.

> The prefrontal cortex helps you postpone gratification. A mighty prefrontal cortex is a must for passing on seconds or walking away from the dessert table.

But you can have a tight, ample brain brake and still behave and eat impulsively. That's because the prefrontal cortex is connected to the visceral brain, seat of the emotional brain. A well-tuned brain brake may not be able to thwart the forces of the visceral brain if your emotions are intense, or red hot. Even the best brakes are overwhelmed by the intense forces of passion.

The Limbic System

The limbic system is the home of desires and passion. It plays a huge role in emotional and unplanned eating. After all, it is part of the visceral brain, home of desires, passions, and the "I-want-it-now" cookie monster! It is located roughly in the center of the brain and is a collective name for a group of structures; key among them are the hypothalamus, hippocampus, amygdala, and thalamus. The limbic system controls appetite, sex drive, playfulness, aggression (amygdala), emotional memories (hippocampus), sleep (thalamus), and smell. It also sets the tone of the brain's positive or negative emotional filters—whether we tend to view the glass as half-full or half-empty— and helps bonding to another person, mother and children, or sexual/romantic partners. With so many key functions in its command and a strong connection to the hypothalamus, the prefrontal cortex, and the frontal lobe, it's no wonder that a healthy limbic system is vital to maintaining a healthy weight.

> The limbic system is the home of desires and passion. It plays a huge role in emotional and unplanned eating.

There is one more peculiar quality about this system: it sees your needs as interchangeable. This sounds simple, but it really has far-reaching consequences for your weight. Any unmet need can be fulfilled by eating. In brain language, your anger, sadness, chronic work or family disappointments, and painful childhood memories are translated into one message: the need for an adequate supply of dopamine, serotonin, and epinephrine (neurotransmitters, or neurochemicals). Emotions reside in the limbic system, and this system uses these neurotransmitters to balance your mood and keep you comfortable. If, for example, you are having a bad day, this part of the brain looks for a way to make you feel good by boosting the necessary neurochemicals. This often equates to eating. But the brain, even the visceral brain, which contains the limbic system, only resorts to the tactic of "robbing Peter to pay Paul" when it has run out of options. If it can't come up with effective solutions to help you get ahead professionally, it can't ignore your depression and frustration, so it defaults to eating comfort foods that will deliver neurotransmitters quickly.

The limbic system wants to restore balance, to make you feel pleasant. If it tries and tries but can't succeed, it does what you do with your cranky child—"Here, eat something." Over time, that translates into lots of extra pounds.

The Basal Ganglia

The basal ganglia are a group of structures mainly associated with movement. Located deep within the brain, they control our physical response to anxiety. One structure, the caudate nucleus, is especially associated with the physical signs of stress and anxiety, such as trembling or fidgeting. The neurochemical imbalances brought on by anxiety or any emotional bump can trigger cravings and overeating as means of soothing and compensating for pleasure shortages.

The Cingulate Gyrus

This area runs along the middle upper part of the brain. Think of it as the brain's gearshift. In order to work smoothly and comfortably, the brain must shift gears according to the task at hand. If you are balancing your checkbook, it shifts to the attention gear, but if you are resting after a long day, it must shift to a lower, relaxation gear. The cingulate is the brain's mechanism for shifting gears from one activity to another. What happens if your brain gets stuck, if the cingulate malfunctions and uses a single gear too often? Your behavior gets stuck. If you are stuck on repetitive worries, your cravings and eating are affected. But the cingulate gyrus influences eating in another way: it creates rigid, strong circuits that connect eating with certain activities, such as driving.

Since everything that affects eating has to do so via the hypothalamus, let's learn a little more about it.

The Hypothalamus

Research findings show consistently that the hypothalamus is the head honcho when it comes to eating. Its function is to regulate metabolic processes, so it's closely connected to the body's ongoing energy needs. When it senses that the body's nutritional requirements are at a low, it signals for food, and because it is connected to the brain's reward system, memory, and motor system, it can get you to move quickly. The hypothalamus has strong connections to the other structures in the limbic system. Thanks to these networks—brain highways— your brain can interchange shortages in any emotional need with eating (we will talk more about this strange brain tendency later in this chapter). Who on this planet hasn't eaten just to feel a little pleasure or to mend a broken heart? The two may seem unrelated to you, but if you were to glance inside a brain in action, you would see the massive, powerful highways that allow it to do so easily—and often.

The Pleasure Arc

We know from studies that track brain neurons that the hypothalamus receives input from the amygdala, the hippocampus, the insula, and the caudate nucleus to prompt eating. This quartet is also involved in eating pleasure; the reason we keep on eating to satisfy our desire rather than nutritional needs. Not coincidentally, these are the same areas that drive cravings for drugs, designer shoes, or endless reruns of *The Sopranos*. These findings suggest that to control your eating, you must invest your time and effort to increase the pleasure and satisfaction in your everyday life from noneating experiences. Extrapolating further, these findings suggest that when it comes to eating some of you would be better off looking at yourselves as recovering addicts. As such, you may find it easier to abstain from certain foods altogether rather than trying to limit foods to which you feel "addicted."

The Dopamine Connection

Further strengthening the connection between pleasure and eating, research shows that food activates the brain's reward system, which in turn releases dopamine, a "feel-good" substance. Dopamine is one of several neurotransmitters secreted in specialized cells inside the brain. Specifically, food activates the pathways running from the midbrain to the nucleus accumbens. When the fibers in those pathways are triggered, dopamine is released. This is what happens when you get the "yum"—the rush of having that piece of chocolate melt in your mouth.

> To control your eating, you must invest your time and effort to increase the pleasure and satisfaction in your everyday life from noneating experiences.

Given this fact, you might think that compulsive overeaters or bingers have more dopamine floating around in their brains than do those who don't routinely overeat, but that doesn't seem to be the case. Using a brain imaging technique know as positron-emission tomography, or PET scan, researchers found a strong correlation between dopamine and body mass index (BMI)—albeit in the "wrong" direction: the more overweight the person, the lower the dopamine levels. What's the story? It seems that all that overeating initially leads to too much dopamine. But as you know, the brain seeks balance above all things, so it has to find a way to lower the high levels of dopamine brought on by overeating. It relies on mechanisms that shut down systems when they routinely produce too much of anything; these mechanisms limit the overabundance of dopamine. The result is observably less dopamine activity in the reward areas of compulsive overeaters' brains than in those of noncompulsive overeaters.

This has tremendous implications. Low dopamine means that many overweight people are walking around, experiencing significantly less pleasure in everyday living than they need to feel calm and comfortable. So the brain does what it can to get a quick dopamine fix. Since eating is an easy method of dopamine delivery and is available just about anytime, it becomes the brain's main source of this chemical. Ideally of course, pleasure should come from both eating and noneating activities: flying a kite, getting a promotion, solving the daily crossword puzzle, and eating a caramel sundae. But the brain has already been trained by sheer repetition to look for food when it needs a dopamine rush, so the vicious cycle starts all over again.

But it doesn't stop there. The brain uses the dopamine rush that comes from eating certain foods for yet another reason: to balance internal imbalances in various functions. Also known as wobbling, or turbulence, eating, really the dopamine that results from eating, is used as a temporary patch not a real solution to repair whatever is causing the imbalance.

Rest assured that the brain doesn't resort to the dopamine fix every time there is a bump in the road, or we would all be dopamine junkies! The brain's first response is to find real solutions to smooth out the wobble and restore balance. To that end, it may shift activity from one location to another, alter the amounts of neurochemicals that are released by different locations, even build new networks, all in an effort to alleviate your discomfort like loneliness, fatigue, rejection, and lack of meaning. In this case the dopamine fix is used as a last resort to keep you from feeling so uncomfortable for so long.

Overeating on Your Mind

It all begins to churn in an unfortunate catch-22 cycle. Studies make it increasingly clear that the quality of the food we eat affects the essence of our core biology. It would be surprising if it did not. After all, our lungs become irritated when we breathe smoke-filled air, our eyes sting when a rogue drop of lemon juice gets squirted into them. So why wouldn't the substances we take into the most visceral parts of our system not interact with our bodies in some way?

The answer is they do interact in significant ways. A new field of research called nutrigenomics tells us that our eating habits—what we eat and how often—can rewire our brain circuitry, sometimes in a matter of hours, by reconfiguring our DNA. Certain foods can turn genes on or off, which can increase or decrease whatever activity these genes are responsible for. Too much or too little of the chemicals the genes produce determines what we eat, how much, and how often. These findings throw linear explanations for weight gain and dieting out the window. I can't imagine that anyone can muster up enough willpower to thwart their own DNA.

> Too much weight can actually dull the senses; erode cognition; and take away the motivation that drives us to be curious, clever, creative, and industrious.

Clearly, unless you quell your eating brain so that it opts for healthy eating, you will continue to crave unhealthy foods. Once inside you, these foods can make it virtually impossible for you to eat healthfully. If you have been eating unhealthy foods for some time, dieting is almost certainly not a solution for you. Your efforts will be better rewarded if you block passage of these "appetizers" and not allow them into your body.

Studies on overweight and obesity make it clear that too much weight—plus certain manufactured ingredients in our food supply—can actually dull the senses; erode cognition; and take away the motivation that drives us to be curious, clever, creative, and industrious. In other words, if you feel that being overweight is hampering your ability to imagine, dream, and achieve, the latest scientific research says you are right. The reasons behind these findings are unclear, but it seems the metabolic disturbances that result from or cause obesity take a toll on young and old brains alike. Young brains that are still developing and not capable of protecting themselves against changes brought on by those ingredients seem especially vulnerable.

The Wobble

While we are not quite certain about all the mechanisms that relay messages to the hypothalamus and turn on the eating switch, we do know that if you're of average weight, chances are your eating brain goes into feeding mode mainly as a result of time elapsed since your last meal—about three to four hours. The reason: you're truly hungry and physiologically in need of food. Your eating brain gets triggered about three times a day, so that's how often you're in feeding mode as well.

If this describes you, you probably have a healthy brain—a well-balanced eating brain—that can handle the occasional imbalance or emotional bump. It can delve into a little comfort food from time to time without putting on any extra pounds, and it can restore equilibrium easily.

But many other people's eating brains get triggered by imbalances several times a day. As a result, they find themselves in the feeding mode almost constantly—thinking about eating, planning a meal or snack, or looking for something to eat. It's logical to assume that eventually all that extra stimulation of the eating brain will lead to overeating and excess weight. And it does.

If this describes you, then your eating brain is most likely prey to a particular danger I call the "wobble." The wobble happens whenever something causes the brain to lose its balance, its inherent dynamic nature. Ever watch a kid send a metal hoop rolling down the street? It rolls straight, fast, and upright for a while, but when the hoop starts to slow down, it begins to wobble. If the kid doesn't catch up to it and give it another push, it will fall.

The brain does virtually the same thing. Maybe you're angry, unhappy, ill at ease, exuberant, confused, distracted; any extreme or excessive dip or rise in mood is a sign of a brain about to lose its smoothly upright performance. As it tries to regain its equilibrium, it starts wobbling all over the place, just like that herky-jerky metal hoop.

We can say that both the hoop and the brain are performing suboptimally—not very efficiently and certainly not effectively. Both are trying to compensate for their loss of performance, to restore the balance they need. In the case of the brain, if it can't restore that balance, it shifts from trying to solve the problem to temporarily distracting itself from it. It is as if the brain has decided it is a waste of energy to go on like this. Since it can't regain equilibrium, it simply takes a break from the pressure of trying to do so and in effect says, "Have something to eat."

Unfortunately, *temporarily* is the operative word. That quick hit of reassurance, soothing, or buffering doesn't deal with the problem; it just sidesteps it for the moment.

My Wobble Test

This test is essential because you can't sit down and have a conversation with your brain. If you could, you might ask it key questions outright: "So tell me, how is it going in there? Are you comfortable? Can you handle all your jobs without feeling drained? Are you getting enough oxygen and nutrients? How about supplies for manufacturing the chemicals that you need to do your job right—got enough? Are you fully in charge of your systems, or are you so overwhelmed that you are letting some things go?"

Since you can't get direct answers to those questions, you must instead look at factors like mood, attention, sleep, physical comfort, and more as your telltale indicators of your brain's strength and performance. That's effectively what you'll do now in the wobble test. It will show you how your wobble is affecting your entire life and how the eating habits that have made you overweight are part of a pattern of suboptimal brain performance. Gaining that understanding will be just the right preparation for the next step, which is understanding how to tweak your brain to improve its performance and lose the weight you want to once and for all.

Answer the following questions based on what's true for you in general. Choose the ranking that most closely describes your experience, and trust your first response. When you've finished, add up your total. The minimum possible score is 40, the maximum is 200.

Take the Test

Legend

1: Very much like me
2: Like me
3: Neutral

4: Unlike me

5: Completely unlike me

1. I feel satisfied and pleasant most of the time. __4__

2. I usually wake up feeling rested. __2__

3. I don't worry about what others think of me. __5__

4. I find it easy to fall asleep. __2__

5. I have a lot of pleasure in my life. __4__

6. I speak softly and slowly. __4__

7. I find life interesting—a big learning experience. __4__

8. I sleep through the night without waking and worrying about the day before or the plans for the day ahead. __4__

9. I can usually control my temper. __2__

10. I quickly get over feeling angry, sad, or hassled. __3__

11. My sadness is usually linked to a life event—a personal setback or the illness or death of a loved one. _____

12. I tend to find the positive in any situation. _____

13. I have achieved a position at work that is in line with what I know my abilities to be. _____

14. I can limit my eating to what I have decided are reasonable amounts and choices. _____

15. I can say that my life is close to my ideal. _____

16. I find time to help others. _____

17. I find it easy to remember what I have just read. _____

18. I am a spiritual person. _____

19. I like playing devil's advocate and thinking of exceptions to or arguments against what someone is saying. _____

20. I plan my actions; I don't act on a whim. _____

21. I look at what's right with a plan before I look at what's wrong. _____

22. I am free of sugar cravings. _____

23. I am free of carbohydrate cravings. _____

24. I maintain a healthy blood pressure. _____

25. I am physically active. _____

26. In general, I have a good memory. _____

27. I am very aware of my surroundings. _____

28. I can comfortably manage what I need to do in a day without feeling overwhelmed or pressured. _____

29. I am strong and healthy. _____

30. I maintain a healthy body weight. _____

31. I am patient when it comes to waiting my turn. _____

32. I stay on-task until I get the job done. _____

33. I prefer doing one thing at a time. _____

34. Things just turn out well for me. _____

35. I have many friends. _____

36. I see the outside world as if through a clean windshield, with clarity and awareness. _____

37. I rarely fret or worry. _____

38. Life is to be explored and enjoyed. _____

39. I am very attentive when I need to be. _____

40. I find it easy to express my feelings. _____

Total _____

Calculate Your Score

0–80: Mild turbulence (Smooth sailing) A smooth, efficient nervous system is typically behind smooth-running lives. In a word, you are likely "thriving." Organized and focused, you set goals and meet them almost effortlessly—or at least it seems so to others, to whom you seem lucky and are an object of admiration. You may be the favorite teacher, parent, or friend who exudes warmth and has the sage advice for someone in need. Whatever your chosen job—chef, forest ranger, software analyst, doctor—you are likely to find joy and fulfillment in the inherent challenges it presents.

You're creative, thinking outside the box to find practical solutions to problems.

An electroencephalogram (EEG) of this state of brain function—a graphic record of the brain's electrical activity, or brainwave frequency, to measure response to stimuli—shows flexibility: the brain puts out all brainwave frequencies without getting stuck in any single gear. Once your system assesses what you need to be doing, it signals the appropriate brain areas to become activated. Once activated, these areas coordinate their efforts and generate optimal neurochemical events to get the job done.

In others words, the brain chooses the optimal frequency gear to shift to depending on the situation or task at hand. If you are in need of sleep, an optimally running brain shifts its activity to the alpha frequency, about eight to twelve cycles per second; then drops to the theta frequency, four to eight cycles per second; and finally to the lowest brainwave frequency, delta frequency, four cycles per second. If you are awake and need to pay attention, your brain shifts to beta frequency, around fourteen cycles per second. It can shift gears freely but can also stay on any single gear for as long as it takes to get a job done; it shows endurance or resiliency.

Emotionally, you may feel satisfied, pleased, blessed, and filled with gratitude and altruism. With a free-flowing, efficient system, you find life's challenges manageable. Being productive is a challenge you meet with enthusiasm, and you usually meet it successfully.

You are likely to be multifaceted, with active social, personal, family, and professional lives. You tend to live in the present; distressing memories and worries over the future don't interfere often or substantively.

You're good at focusing on a specific task, which makes you a great listener as well. And because your system can perform well enough to get everything done, you have extra energy for rest or play. In effect, your brain provides whatever is needed for a smooth, calm, serene, mentally lucid life.

Where weight management is concerned, weight gain may come from social overeating—two or more restaurant meals per week. You may also be eating too much healthy food, which could result in excess weight especially in middle and later life. But for the most part, you're able to exercise balance between bottom-up and top-down thinking and confine your eating to self-imposed restrictions. If you wobble, it's temporary, a transition, and you can return to your baseline fairly easily. Your weight is manageable.

For you, weight management is a question of recognizing danger zones and reframing your life's transitions—from work to home to social engagement to work, and so on—without relying on food to cushion the awkwardness of the temporary turbulence. You'll likely focus your brain-fitness training on enhancing or optimizing your brain's flexibility so that it becomes even better able to shift from one state to another.

81–120: Medium turbulence (A bit bumpy) Even a perfectly engineered system has its flaws, and the brain is no exception. Your daily functioning depends on whether your score is at the upper or lower limit of the range and on how attuned you are to fluctuations in your energy and mood. Mild turbulence may have little impact on your everyday life. What impact it has most likely shows up during times of transitioning or periods of stress. For example, you may have trouble going to sleep after a late night at the office or an emotional meeting with a family member or friend. Or you may have difficulty reentering the workplace after a vacation—even after a weekend. Sometimes the turbulence shows up just from reentering your home and rejoining your family after work. It may manifest as irritability ("Why are all the lights on in the house? Why is the TV so loud?"). You may also find that you are vulnerable to using food inappropriately during such transitions. Emotionally raw from the reentering stress, you reach inside the refrigerator for ice cream or leftovers before calming down enough to plan out the next meal. Typically, this type of eating is done while you're standing up, still dressed in work clothes or clothes you've been in for most of the day, and still not quite acclimated to the environment you have just entered.

Mild turbulence is also likely to impact your eating during times of excessive pressure—if, for example, you find yourself taking care of a sick family member or adapting to a new job. Since connecting to life events and emotions is sluggish, the joy and satisfaction inherent in just being alive may be compromised. Some people look to food, alcohol, or multiple relationships in their search for balance and comfort from this state. After all, if reality is not rewarding, why not shift to something that is rewarding? Food is an easy feel-good solution that's effortless and private. You don't need cooperation from another person. "Food can't say no to me," as one compulsive overeater put it. Of course, when the weight adds up, the overeater feels worse, but when you're starving for pleasant sensations or feeling emotionally raw, who thinks of consequences? Escape from distress is the number-one priority.

Since mild turbulence means nearly daily discomfort or disruption, there is little time to rest and recoup. The calm, healing day that can undo the distress and eating of yesterday or last week never comes. The system spends nearly all its time looking for that soothing and calming solution to balance the negative emotional states. Typically, it finds it in the no-brainer default—eating, especially high-calorie comfort foods. The ability to exercise cognitive restraint consistently may be limited, while emotional and uncontrollable eating becomes more prominent.

121–160: Serious turbulence (Hold on!) Chances are your system is wobbling a lot as it tries to compensate for being out of equilibrium. Think of this type of disturbance as a mild mental fog that keeps you from being fully tuned in to what's around you. You are functioning but not thriving.

With this score, your turbulence is present almost daily and affects many areas of your life. You may find you cannot focus on something long enough to finish it.

The EEG pattern of this wobble will show maladaptive patterns, like being "stuck" in a certain frequency or gear. You may be stuck on high (beta frequency) or low (delta frequency), neither of which is desirable. It's just like when you exercise your legs without also doing upper-body work; the result is the less overall fitness. Nor can you easily tell if you are trapped in a low or high frequency. People with low frequencies can appear depressed or agitated and hyper, whereas people stuck in high gear can appear sleepy and depressed.

Sleep may be affected. You wake up way too early or have trouble falling asleep at night. Both sleep and wakefulness suffer; each intrudes on the other. You sort of sleepwalk through daily life; the brain's dominant brainwave patterns may be more indicative of sleep than of wakefulness. This is a huge constraint on everything you do. Here's how one mother of three described it: "I'm on automatic—going through the motions. I go through the day just functioning. I pick up the kids, and I drop them off. I do what I need to do. I'm tired of the same routine. If I stop and think about how I'm feeling or my needs, I'm afraid I will run away."

Serious discomfort usually means serious overeating to soothe the discomfort. Sleep disruption alone can contribute over 20 percent to your weight! When in serious wobble you may find yourself barely having enough energy to get through the day—who has time to shop and prepare healthy food and when it comes down to it, who cares? Weight may be one more nagging chronic pain on top of many. Eating on "automatic" can also mean that whole bags or plates of food disappear while thinking or preoccupied with something else. However, you still recognize your weight gain as unhealthy and may have solid plans to do something about it when life's responsibilities ease up a bit.

161–200: Severe turbulence (Help!) Your brain is working hard to cushion you from reality. To do so, it shifts to a lower level of awareness, a brain activity pattern that some neuroscientists equate with whistling in a graveyard. Simply put, you're trying to keep yourself from being scared out of your wits.

Your system has lost its balance, and the physical and emotional symptoms, disorganization, and distress associated with this severe wobbling can be life-limiting and incapacitating. You probably find it difficult to keep up with the demands of everyday life without feeling exhausted and emotionally raw.

The EEG pattern here shows severe constraints: frequencies that are too high, too low, or unstable (fluctuating wildly between high and low). You are likely to have difficulty breaking loose from repetitive thinking, negative emotions, and unhealthy eating routines. If you are stuck on a negative feeling, person, or routine, chances are your brain is too. I might also add that any self-defeating behavior is a telltale sign of internal struggle between your bottom-up thinking that's looking for a quick good time and your top-down, logical side. You will benefit by engaging in more behaviors that boost the reflective brain, such as pausing before acting; calculating costs and benefits of all options; and giving and accepting higher-level emotions like kindness, respect, and altruism.

As to weight management, there is no such thing. Where food is concerned, emotional eating and uncontrollable cravings and urges can be so intense that they overwhelm your ability to show consistent cognitive restraint. Many people with this level of turbulence have diabetes, high blood pressure, arrhythmia, skin conditions, and gastrointestinal problems—the typical stress-related disorders. Many are treated with psychotropic medications and psychotherapy. But the truth is that these treatments won't be entirely successful unless maladaptive brain patterns are changed to restore balance.

Often, the person with a severe wobble will work hard to keep up the appearance of being together and happy—just like everyone else at the party—while pushing her real feelings into the background. The conflict between appearance and the reality of the person's inner emotional state can generate serious anxiety and chronic lack of energy, and lead to even more inappropriate eating.

Tough as it may be to confront your wobble, this test should have given you some idea of what this global dysregulation is doing to your life and specifically to your weight. Now that you know, what are you going to do about it? What *can* you do about it? Before you move on to the next chapter and learn which part of your brain is causing your wobble, let's expose your enemies so that it's clear what you're up against.

Fighting the Foodscape

You won't find the word *foodscape* in any dictionary, but I'll wager you know precisely what I mean. I'm talking about all those external cues in our environment that get us to eat: fast-food establishments on every corner offering supersized portions of high-calorie, high-fat fried foods. Highly stylized, Technicolor images of food that make our mouths water. A language and culture of eating that are highly sexualized, morality based, and peppered with idioms of substance abuse. Chocolate molten cake is a sin. Apple pie is an indulgence. And what's that sound you make as you sink your teeth into a piece of cheesecake? That's a moan of gratification by any definition. The foodscape artists read your dopamine nature and loaded up the foodscape with irresistible eating. In a collision-course fashion, consider this: the brain evolved historically to view fats and sweets as both sparse and valuable, if not vital to survival. You don't need to go further to see why we are all in danger of becoming overweight—brain looking for dopamine, which is plentiful in fatty, sweet foods meets modern foodscape.

The brain is not stupid; it's just operating under guidelines that are no longer valid. Evolutionarily speaking, there was no need for internal off switches, because the food often simply ran out. There was no point in having brain mechanisms that curbed humans' desire for foods that helped keep them alive and healthy. As a result, the eating brain's survival strategy, which is still very much a part of us today, was to eat a lot and to focus on high-calorie foods.

Now that you know something about your brain's nature and its obsolete wiring, fast forward to the modern foodscape. Can you see disaster unfolding? Not only does the food keep coming, but today's foodscape actually invites us to eat more and more. Making matters worse, the brain's reliance on sensory "evidence" to decide if it's had enough is undermined by the foodscape: dozens of chicken-wing bones are quickly removed, and a new clean plate tells your brain, "Eating has just begun" (for the fourth time in thirty minutes).

Supersizing is another way of undermining the brain's ability to know when you've had enough. A dish of ice cream seems about right as long as it's packed to the rim of the dish. The brain seems just as satisfied with eight ounces as it is with sixteen; as long as it fills the dish all the way up!

The foodscape has yet another way of fooling the brain: high-calorie foods! Remember, we usually eat for about the same length of time, about twenty minutes, at each meal. Our ancestors had to chew long and hard to fill their stomachs to their stretching/breaking points (as long as forty-five minutes), just to take in 400 calories. In the modern foodscape, you can easily take in 3,000 calories, most of them fat, in one short sitting. High-calorie foods take up so little space in the stomach that you can practically eat them all day without ever feeling too full. Consider that many of today's foodscapes offer nothing but highly caloric foods; think of food courts in shopping malls and streets with one of each of the well-known fast-food chains in a row.

Foods with high calorie content are huge factors behind obesity, but when they are combined with some manufactured nutrients they give eating an almost surreal twist. These foods can rewire the brain in a way that makes food cravings as intense and difficult to resist as cocaine or alcohol. The food industries behind the modern foodscape may not set out to get you hooked on these foods; all they care about is that you keep coming back for more. Great news for their bottom line, not so great for your bottom line.

> In a very real sense, the brain is a victim of its own success. It didn't figure that we would invent ways to travel great distances without moving a limb, to do so with lightning speed, and to have our food brought to us en route.

In a very real sense, the brain is a victim of its own success. It didn't figure that we would invent ways to travel great distances without moving a limb, to do so with lightning speed, and to have our food brought to us en route. No wonder the brain finds itself out of sync with the modern foodscape; it's suffering a time lag, and your waistline is paying the price.

It all makes for a foodscape filled with a number of risk factors operating at the same time. Add to these multiple risks the brain's innate habit of feeding you to balance life's ouches, and you can see that you are confronting a very substantive challenge when you set out to lose weight—especially if you set out to lose weight by dieting.

Fighting the Wobble

Brain wobbling is a telltale sign of brain instability or loss of efficiency. As a result of this instability, emotional, physical, and metabolic systems are also off balance. The degree of wobbling reflects the nature of the emotional bump and the hardiness of your particular system.

The idea that a central brain wobble is behind excessive weight gain came about as a way to explain research studies that show that excessive eating and weight rarely happen in isolation. Obesity correlates with negative mood, poor sleep, metabolic abnormalities, and problems with learning and memory. What's the connection between wobbling and overeating?

Remember that the brain is a superbly adaptable and flexible organ. When an insult causes it to wobble, it reacts quickly to restore balance. In its infinite wisdom, it unleashes a multitude of sophisticated operations all geared to regain its equilibrium. It shifts activity from one brain location to another and triggers changes in the release and effectiveness of neurochemicals and hormones.

The causes of wobbles are many.

Entanglement with Food

Emotions are intimately interwoven with the eating brain. Thanks to the strong connections between areas of the emotional brain and the eating brain, a strong bout of anger can push blood into the stomach lining, increase its mobility, and trigger hunger all at the same time. When you are so mad that you "see red," blood rushes to your gastrointestinal tract so your stomach turns red and ready for something to eat.

Mood disorders are commonly associated with imbalances in neurotransmitters as well as obesity. This link between mood, neurotransmitter imbalances, and weight gain is understandable given the connections between the limbic system (emotional brain) and the eating brain. How can feelings cause you to gain weight? Negative emotions lead to imbalances in dopamine, serotonin, and epinephrine. These imbalances interfere with the body's ability to keep track of how much you are eating, so it doesn't stop eating when you've had enough. Not only that, but these imbalances cause cravings for sweets and comfort foods, which further aggravate weight gain.

The brain as a system senses if you've had enough and should stop calling for more food, but the eating brain is very self-indulgent and self-gratifying; it can override the reflective brain because it's looking for a good time. The eating brain hooks up to the brain's reward system forming the eating pleasure arc discussed earlier.

Your Calorie Savings Account

Your eating brain is certainly behind each brownie and caramel sundae you eat, but that shouldn't make it your instant enemy. It's just using old guidelines (see the section "Fighting the Foodscape" earlier in the chapter for more information), so it thinks it's getting you healthier while actually it's slowly killing you. Because of those old guidelines, if at the end of the day you have some leftover calories from the foods you ate, it doesn't direct your body to burn it off, like dumping of extra jet fuel (wouldn't that be sweet!). Instead, it delegates those calories to turn into fat around your waist.

The modern eating brain has retained the tendency to save leftover energy (in the form of fat) whenever possible and to make more fat when you are under stress and life is full of difficulties. The stress hormone cortisol can trigger the eating brain even when you are not hungry. The brain is not trying to add to your troubles; in fact, it's trying to see that you stay healthy by making sure you don't starve. As far as the eating brain is concerned, hardship means potential food shortages ahead, so it deposits more fat when it senses impending doom. Remember, nature didn't tear down the old brain, it built on top of it (see Chapter 1). That means your visceral brain, which evolved when food supplies were limited, is still calling the shots.

Smell Triggers

The smell of food can also activate the eating brain—even when you're satiated—simply because that smell reminds you of happy times. That's because the eating brain is well connected to the hippocampus where emotional memories of eating that food are stored. In an instant, you remember how good it felt the last time you ate whatever food it is that you are smelling. Now you know why a cheese smell is pumped into the frequented fruit section of the grocery store—to ensure that you pass by the cheese section.

Lack of Exercise

We would be lucky, and it would be highly unusual, if we could walk or pedal to one errand a day. Our modern lifestyle discourages walking or biking in the course of carrying out our daily jobs and has also caused a shortage in safe, clean green spaces where we can get exercise. Lazy muscles in your body can signal a lazy brain in your head or giving in to cravings for more food.

The Protector Myth

"If this were dangerous, there would be a fence here!" my then-seven-year-old daughter, Andria, cried matter-of-factly as she was headed down a cliff—all because she was trying to avoid a bee. Even at that young age, the message of an outside "protector" was already second nature to her. Part of the reason for overweight is overreliance on government and society to protect us from harm. This may be true in some areas, but it would be a costly mistake to extend this belief to the foods you eat.

Far from protecting you, the government has actually helped create fast-food campaigns aimed at getting you to eat more unhealthy foods. The FDA is an agency responsible for setting dietary guidelines and maintaining balance between food supply and consumption. However, in 2003 it found itself with tons of surplus cheese sitting in its warehouses. Driven to boost consumption of the surplus cheese, the FDA joined forces with the food chain Wendy's. Together they created ways to increase the amount of cheese to existing, or add it to new, menu items. The ad campaign "summers of cheese" was successful in "discarding" the surplus cheese; shifting it from warehouses to . . . your waistline.

The tension between political and economic forces and consumer health has a longer past. For example, during the Ford era in the '70s palm oil or "rat oil" as it was better known until then, found its way into American supermarkets and became one of the most ubiquitous vegetable oil substitutes. Palm oil was imported from Malaysia for wide use in U.S. food products for two main reasons: it is far cheaper than corn oil and was a political necessity because of political arrangements between the U.S. department of agriculture and Malaysia. What's wrong with palm oil?

Palm oil or "rat oil" as it was known until the '70s, is high in saturated fat, the kind of fat that builds up along arteries increasing the risk of high blood pressure, heart disease, and premature death. Palm oil is 45 percent saturated compared to pig fat, which is 38 percent saturated. It was nonetheless imported from Malaysia and included in U.S. food products in the '70s for political reasons, despite protests from scientists and U.S. farmers. The food industry is a giant contributor (12 percent) to this consumer-driven economy and employs 17 percent of the labor force. The economy benefits from over-consumption of food, overweight (new industries that cater to greater girths), and even your weight-loss efforts and poor health. The protector myth fuels unhealthy eating by creating an air of false security about the foods you eat.

Another example for staying on your guard when it comes to the type of foods you choose relates to high fructose corn syrup (HFCS). It is a corn-based sweetener, cheaper than sugar but six times sweeter than sugar, that found its way into U.S. foods under questionable circumstances. But, unlike white sugar (dextrose or sucrose), that undergoes a meta-bolic breakdown before reaching organs like the liver, HFCS arrives at the liver intact. The liver then engages in some-thing called *metabolic shunting*. The net result is that HFCS replacement of sugar means more sugar in your metabolic system. This effect is suspected to be behind the growing problem in the U.S. with insulin resistance and metabolic syndrome: obesity, heart disease, and diabetes. But it's hard to find food product that does not contain HFCS. In fact, it found its way in to my organic whole-wheat loaf of bread! HFCS is cheaper than sugar and helps food look good longer so it is here to stay.

And let's not forget that in January 2004, the U.S. govern-ment came out against the guidelines by the World Health Organization (WHO) to curb obesity worldwide. The WHO plan called for, among other things, limiting processed foods and foods high in fat and sugar. It also called for people to eat more fruits and vegetables and to keep sugar to about 10 percent of a person's daily caloric intake. Under pressure from the powerful sugar industry the Department of Health and Human Services failed to endorse the WHO recommendations.

The bottom line: stay skeptical about ingredients that you don't understand and decide for yourself if a food helps you thrive.

No Brakes

Foodscape eating cues are only part of the story behind overeating. Along with constantly being bombarded with images and smells of food as part of the daily foodscape, the brain's brake system is also part of the problem; it may be getting sluggish as the foodscape cues become increasingly powerful. The brain brake is part of the reflective brain—the area where we plan, organize, and reflect on our deeds before we act. This mechanism gives us the ability to drive *by* and not *through* the fast-food restaurant.

In recent years, we have become more likely than previous generations to give in to many if not all of our basic desires, not just food pleasure. We indulge our primal urges for lust, violence, envy, and sexuality as never before. The bottom-up influence on our actions, the visceral brain, is getting a workout, and as a result, it's getting stronger, while the top-down influence of the reflective brain is getting weaker. Fortified, the cookie-monster part of our nature is gaining strength and can easily override any resistance by the brain brake. The fact that overindulging in areas other than eating fuels cravings for food even more may be a surprise to you. But, given the layout of the eating brain it's entirely predictable.

The Overweight Majority

It's truly difficult to feel overweight when you are surrounded by others who weigh as much as or more than you do! After all, we judge size on relative terms. An ant is small compared to you but appears gigantic to a paramecium. As more Americans become overweight, it's getting more difficult to tell exactly how overweight we truly are—and if we are. Another consequence of the overweight majority has to do with social pressure as an agent for change. Take how the United States as a society collectively progressed from viewing smoking as the epitome of glamour to the current view of it as an ugly killer. Social sanctions impose pressure to change behavior above and beyond the inherent negative impact on health: smoking and excess weight can make you sick and even shorten your lifespan, but for some, being looked down on is more of a reason to control or change behavior.

Not Enough Sleep

Sleep deprivation more than doubles the risk of obesity in children and adults. Studies of overweight children show that kids ages five to ten who sleep fewer than ten hours a night are three to five times more likely to be overweight than children who sleep twelve or more hours per night. Sleep was even more dominant in predicting obesity than other powerful factors such as parental education and socioeconomic level, TV viewing, or the amount of regular physical activity. The fewer hours spent sleeping, the greater the amount of excess weight.

According to researchers at the University of Chicago, sleep deprivation leads to increases in hormones that regulate hunger and cravings for rich foods. Clearly, there's a correlation between body weight and the amount of sleep a person gets, and hours of sleep can be a predictor of overweight or obesity in children and adults.

These findings lend support to the global dysregulation hypothesis: body weight is not the only thing the brain seems to mishandle. Sleep, emotion, and even cognition—the ability to learn and think clearly—suffer at the same time. The fact that children are affected further suggests that turbulence that disturbs the brain's central mechanisms manifests itself very early on in inappropriate sleeping and eating.

Insufficient Pleasure

Clearly, an intensely damaging, internal event (or "insult") seems to precede imbalances in numerous functions. This suggests that the insult disrupts the brain's ability to maintain a healthy balance in several of its key functions. Weight gain is the most obvious symptom because it is so readily observable. Most people would seek help to manage their weight, but few recognize poor sleep or persistent "blahs" as coexisting conditions.

Have you ever tried to calm a crying baby? You can rock him, walk him up and down, take him for a drive in the car, stand on your head and make funny noises. Nothing works until finally you just give him a bottle or a breast. Ahhhh. He's not crying now.

But of course, for either infant or grown-up, this solution of last resort is not really a solution at all; it's just an interim stopgap to make us feel comfortable—or at least less uncomfortable. This mechanism is hardwired; there is little you can do to eliminate it. What you can do is help your brain regain its ability to regulate all of your functions, so it can put out fires in remote stations without sounding the alarm to eat. Help your brain thrive all the time, not just default to temporary solutions, and it can help you lose weight.

Otherwise, you're simply confronting the foodscape with the odds against you and one hand tied behind your back.

The Wobble Cure

In the upcoming chapters, you'll condition your brain to fight its global wobble, focusing on fitness in the areas of your particular wobble, the one that prompts you to eat, overeat, and gain weight. You'll retrain your brain to a new level of fitness so that it performs at its peak. An optimally performing brain is one that can recover quickly from any wobble without resorting to inappropriate eating. It's a brain that can keep you as trim, as fit, as lean and efficient as it is. That's what you're after.

To confront the foodscape, to challenge it successfully, and to triumph over it, you will need to start with your brain. Now you understand how your brain works, and how and why it wobbles. In the rest of this book, you'll learn where in your eating brain your wobble comes from and precisely how to retrain your brain so that you deal with that wobble in a whole different way.

PART 2

Reframe

The Second Step

Reframing the Way You Think

Here comes the exciting part. Now you're going to find out which part of your eating brain is likely to be triggering your wobble. You already glanced into your brain's general health by taking the wobble test; now you will learn more details about what your brain is doing well and not so well.

These efforts to assess your brain's overall function as well as zero in on specific trouble spots are meant to show you a window into your own inner world—the behind-the-scenes brain activity that happens while you are busy putting food in your mouth. Perhaps it's *literally* true that no one puts food in your mouth; strangers don't typically force-feed you. But what about the strange subparts of you? Those splintered selves sure feel like they are behind the third and fourth snack attack. The wobble test and self-tests later in this chapter will give you a name for the culprit that may actually be "forcing" you to eat. And not just healthy food, but fat, sweet, low-fiber food.

First, let's see how you can use the results from the wobble test to identify the old explanations you gave yourself and perhaps others for your weight gain. Then you will have a chance to reframe these explanations. See how overeating fits into your overall brain function.

Upgrade Your Framework: Reframe

To *reframe* means to change old ideas and explanations about overeating to new ones. You may not know it, but you already see your overeating and weight gain within a framework. In other words, consciously or not, you have "framed" your understanding of overeating in a way that makes the best sense given the information available to you.

To remind yourself of your existing framework, think of those conversations you have with yourself as you proceed to eat beyond what you think is sensible or healthy: "I have no self-control. I'm too lazy. I'm too busy to worry about my weight." Take a look at your inner thoughts and feelings while you're overeating and especially afterward, and you will see that you are indeed using some type of framework that lets you understand your actions. Whether it's valid or dead wrong, helpful or not, you keep the framework because it gives you a reason for that black box, the "yawning gap" between your intentions and your actions.

Since the current weight-loss culture is linear and insists on treating overeating by focusing on the eating itself, chances are you have framed your overeating to fit that model. Now that you have information about how the brain can contribute to an uncontrollable drive to eat you have the opportunity to reframe the old—I might say, obsolete—linear ideas for a more accurate upgrade.

Reframing lets you see the true causes of your overeating, and when we talk about root causes of any of our actions, all roads lead to the brain. Finding that your brain's function or wobble plays a role in your overeating and weight gain is an important new reframing piece. Hopefully, you will never again think of overeating without thinking about your brain and consider how well the rest of you is doing.

Another reframing piece comes from knowing the part of the brain that's "acting out" the most. This piece of information will enable you to personalize the brain training plan so that it targets the part of your brain that needs the most help. If, for instance, you find that your brain brake—the prefrontal cortex—is weak or sluggish you can specially target exercises in Chapter 6 that help build this muscle. I say *specially*, because you should focus on all areas to build overall brain fitness. Just as you can't improve your overall physical fitness by always sitting on a bench and working on your biceps while ignoring your lower body, cardiovascular fitness, and flexibility, it is physically impossible to improve brain fitness by boosting only one brain area and its function.

> Reframing lets you see the true causes of your overeating, and when we talk about root causes of any of our actions, all roads lead to the brain.

How Reframing Works

Laura is a forty-eight-year-old mom. Married to Jim for twenty years and the mother of a daughter, Caroline, and a son, Andrew, she began to gain weight in her early forties. By the time she came to me for consultation, she was about thirty pounds overweight. Although Laura dieted from time to time, losing a few pounds each time before gaining it all back, she was convinced that the weight gain was a function of middle age. "It's natural," she insisted. "Everybody my age puts on weight. There's no rhyme or reason to it."

Most of the weight gain, she conceded, had come from a fairly recent tendency to binge on high-calorie junk food and sweets. Laura explained this particular craving as "hormonal"— a taste shift experienced by all perimenopausal women.

At least, that's what Laura claimed until she went through the first step of the OPT program, the wobble test you took back in Chapter 2. She was surprised by the level of turbulence reflected in her high wobble score; she had become so used to her symptoms that she thought of them as normal parts of herself.

As we talked, Laura was able to identify three basic reasons for the imbalance that had set her brain wobbling: the members of her family. Caroline, sixteen years old, had been showing signs of an eating disorder for two years. Her husband, Jim, was completely uncommunicative—about the issue with Caroline or anything else. And Andrew's response to all of this was simply to flee the family as often as he could for as long as he could. Laura was left looking at each individual family member's trouble and being overwhelmed by it—helpless, frustrated, and chronically agitated.

For Laura, those feelings of frustration and agitation had triggered widespread disturbances in key brain mechanisms. They were the insult to her brain that sent it into a wobble. Although she had a great deal of turmoil in her life, she held her weight as the problem she needed help with. She didn't even think of mentioning other worrisome trends that had cropped up about the same time as the changes to her eating habits: she didn't feel like exercising, found excuses to get out of meeting her friends, was unusually quiet in her own thoughts most of the time, woke up feeling tired most mornings, let the housekeeping go, and watched more TV than ever.

Laura is typical of many people who seek help with weight management. She had unconsciously framed her eating changes to fit popular misconceptions about weight gain. She didn't consider her other problems in connection with her eating. She framed her weight gain in terms of cultural and popular belief: when you gain weight, focus on your eating. Laura simply followed the guidelines of the long-standing, acceptable dogma that supposes a linear connection between overeating on one hand and weight gain on the other.

She justified giving in to her unhealthy cravings. After all, her family was falling apart; this was no time for her to take care of the finer things in life like working out. Self-care became a luxury she could not invest in; she closed her ears to her own needs and made her family her priority. With bigger things to worry about than her own well-being, eating pleasure was the bright spot in her day. How could she deprive herself of the one thing that still made her feel good?

Little did she know that her brain was reacting in the same way. With so much happening, much of it unhappy, her brain gave up on its own upkeep. Who has the energy to regenerate new cells to replace the ones that died because of, among other things, Laura's poor diet and stress? Her brain gave up on maintaining and improving itself because it could hardly keep up with the demands that her wobble was making. Weight gain was just one consequence of its troubles.

Armed with the "snapshot" of her brain's activity, Laura zoomed in on her brain and reframed her increased desire and taste for "junky, crunchy snack foods." She saw that her emotional upheaval weakened her willingness and ability to impose cognitive restraint—to put the brakes on unhealthy snacking. She came to see her constant cravings as part of a whole cascade of imbalances. Poor sleep, no exercise, and unhealthy eating meant more irritability and low energy, which in turn triggered cravings that led her to feel even more despair, which in turn led to even greater imbalances in her brain's mechanisms and even less sleep, less exercise, greater irritability, and less energy. Laura's eating brain did just what it was prewired to do; it triggered the feeding mode, prompting her to eat inappropriately and excessively.

Once Laura saw that, she understood her overeating and weight gain in the context of what was happening inside her brain, not in the context of yielding to cravings out of moral weakness or passively accepting a normal hormonal change.

She reframed her perception of why she was overweight, and this reframing enabled her to zero in on the retraining she would have to use to bypass, resist, or control her urge to overeat or to eat inappropriately.

> Once you reframe your eating by seeing just where and how the conversation between you and the splintered parts of your brain breaks down, you'll be able to retrain those parts of your brain.

Knowing that your overeating is tied to wobbling is already light-years away from other weight-loss approaches. But you can upgrade the "snapshot" with a "close-up" that lets you home in on a more detailed map of your brain. The second step of the OPT program is aimed at locating the specific part of the brain where your imbalance resides and identifying the nature of the malfunction that needs to be fixed.

Once you reframe your eating by seeing just where and how the conversation between you and the splintered parts of your brain breaks down, you'll be able to retrain those parts of your brain. Result? Your system won't default to eating when confronted by its wobble, no matter how turbulent the circumstances.

How Reframing Can Help You with Weight Loss

Once you see overeating and weight gain as equivalent to brain imbalances, the paradigm automatically shifts. But how do you do that?

First, you take the self-tests in this chapter. It might appear that the questions have nothing to do with eating; they don't ask you about how much or how often you eat. In fact, the items are simply asking you if you are generally comfortable and satisfied living your daily life. But make no mistake; these questions have everything to do with your excessive desire for food. They reveal telltale signs about what may be happening inside your head. Your responses can help pinpoint the possible culprits to your overeating—brain areas that have lost their balance.

How is this possible? In the ongoing effort to map the brain, scientists have identified and continue to identify the function of every brain site. These efforts have led to brain maps that can pinpoint a function to a specific location. A symptom can often be translated into a malfunction or impairment of one or more brain areas. If, for instance, you consistently fidget, feel on edge, and dread public speaking, the area inside your brain known as the basal ganglia (the center for fidgetiness) is probably overactive. What else do you do when you fidget or feel pressured? Getting the munchies is an all-too-well-known side effect.

Next, let's assume that you come to attribute much of your overeating to an overactivity in the fidgetiness center. Reframing helps you manage your eating by treating the root cause— anxiety, shakiness, and muscular tension. The next logical step is to look into information about how to manage that anxiety: a walk, a massage, a phone call or visit with a reassuring friend, psychotherapy, or a yoga or tai chi class.

Notice how reframing can help you treat your fidgetiness without the munchies! Reframing helps you shift your efforts to find solutions for your anxiety problem. Instead of using dopamine and other feel-good chemicals delivered by high-calorie foods to soothe your basal ganglia, you problem solve and find effective, lasting solutions.

Okay, even if you don't believe for a minute that you will do the logical thing and address your tension with healthy solutions instead of sedating yourself with food, chances are information about the root causes of overeating can still help you. Once you learn those causes, you can't unlearn them; awareness alone is a huge factor in helping control overeating.

Reframing and Internal Causes of Overeating

There are four basic categories of eating triggers: the body's need for refueling; external foodscape cues; internal emotional cues; and finally, the combination of internal emotional cues and external foodscape eating cues.

Reframing is especially vital for curbing emotional eating. That's because most of the eating behind weight gain is considered to be triggered by internal states, such as emotion, fatigue, sleepiness, and other inner turmoil. You already learned in previous chapters about the brain's tendency to meet shortages in one area by compensating in another (or "robbing Peter to pay Paul"). The same applies to the limbic system's reactions: one craving is pretty much like another. Even though to your reflective brain, the things you crave may be wildly different from one another, all cravings—whether for food, sex, tranquillity, power, or excitement—are controlled by structures that collectively make up the limbic system.

You can use the brain's own tendency to reframe and meet your food craving (need) with a healthier one. Since the physical experience of a craving is pretty much the same, be it food, sex, or an orgiastic shopping spree, use your imagination and satisfy one that doesn't involve calories.

What you're doing is reframing the meaning of your cravings. It's all a matter of interpretation—if you think your craving for a brownie can only go away by eating a brownie, think again. Your brain is asking for pleasure, stimulation, escape, or distraction. Why bake brownies to satisfy the desire when you know that the brain is wired to receive just as much pleasure from a number of noncaloric choices? "Feed" your brain those pleasures, and over time, it will rewire itself to crave these activities instead of brownies. The more times you deliver noncaloric pleasure to the brain when it "calls" for a brownie, the less it will think of brownies.

> If you think your craving for a brownie can only go away by eating a brownie, think again.

In other words, your seemingly insatiable urge for food is not vastly different from a simultaneous craving to see your old pal John. You can put your energy into arranging a meeting with John, and you may (1) be distracted from ruminating about food and (2) still give your brain what it needs on the emotional front. Getting together with John can thus reduce the tension in your brain, help it restore its chemical or electrical imbalance, and—as an added bonus—lessen the intensity of your food cravings. You give in to your noncaloric cravings instead of to your food cravings.

Repetition is key to rewiring your brain. If you substitute golf with John for today's food craving, a walk in the woods for tomorrow's food craving, and a visit to the gym for the food craving the day after, you may begin to create a new sequence of responses to those cravings. The more you repeat the sequence, the easier it is to do and the stronger the sequence becomes.

How? Think of your brain as similar to your MP3 player; that is, it keeps a record of what you listen to most often, and those songs automatically dominate the default playlist the MP3 sets up. The more you "play" nonfood pleasures to satisfy limbic needs, the more likely your brain will be to default to them automatically and the less likely it will be to play your old tune of unhealthy eating patterns.

Right now, your brain may be stuck on the brownie playlist, assuming that eating brownies makes you feel emotionally, physically, and cognitively fit. Okay, you've played that tune—"feeling down = eating brownies"—too often in the past, and your brain is stuck on it. So change the playlist by choosing new tunes to default to. Each time you make a healthy choice, you strengthen your brain's pathways to feeling emotionally, physically, and cognitively fit through body pleasure rather than through brownies. In time, those healthy pleasures will dominate the playlist, and that's where your internal MP3 will go when there's a bump in the emotional road.

> Each time you make a healthy choice, you strengthen your brain's pathways to feeling emotionally, physically, and cognitively fit.

Let's proceed to the tests that will let you reframe what you've learned about wobbles into terms specific to your brain. Then we can design a retraining program that will include both general brain fitness exercises and spot-conditioning exercises for your particular imbalance.

Take Aim: Reframe

Back in Chapters 1 and 2, we took a look at the brain in general and at the eating brain in particular. We explored some of the complexities of the brain and talked about both its power to regulate our weight and it's powerlessness to keep weight off once a wobble is in place. You learned that your brain has its own unique architecture, built out of your genetic heritage, your environment, your experience, even your personality. As

Figure 3-1

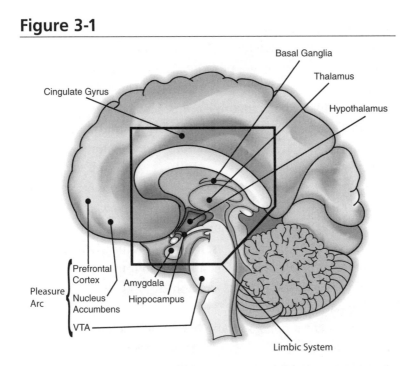

Brain sliced down the middle showing the five brain locations linked to emotional overeating and pleasure-driven or "addictive" eating.

we mentioned in Chapter 2, there are at least five brain locations or structures that are easily observable, leave telltale signs on eating patterns, and can have a particularly profound impact on eating habits. They're the prefrontal cortex, the limbic system, the basal ganglia, the cingulate gyrus, and the pleasure arc or reward system.

The *prefrontal cortex* (the brain's brake), along with the frontal lobe, is where the brain carries out "executive functions" such as self-reflection, consideration of different courses of action, planning, calculation, and imagination. The last area to reach maturity—it takes until our midtwenties—it helps curb impulsive behavior. It's easy to guess the positive consequences of a robust braking system: it allows for pausing and considering consequences. When the prefrontal cortex malfunctions, one possible symptom can be out-of-control behavior or difficulty pausing before taking action, like not being able to pause and consider your eating options before delving into that caramel sundae. It's the area that helps you "think before you leap" instead of impulsively moving full speed ahead and facing negative consequences later. The brain's all-important brake muscle is located in this area. When strong and well connected to the rest of your engine (other brain structures), you can make healthy eating choices—at least most of the time. Underactivity in the prefrontal cortex has been linked to impulse control disorders and behaviors such as alcoholism, risky sexual behavior, and drug addiction.

You've met the *limbic system* before; it's the cookie-monster part of your brain and the seat of your emotions. Problems or instability in this system can mean that your emotions rule your eating. The most common internal triggers for overeating are located in limbic structures.

The *basal ganglia,* or fidgetiness center, is where tension resides. Instability here can lead to eating for something to do or to escape jitteriness and nerves.

The *cingulate gyrus* is the brain's flexibility on/off switch. Think of it as the switch for fluidity, or "gnarliness"—how open you are to changes in routine. When the switch isn't working well, your eating can fall into bad or unhealthful habits and rituals. Overactivity in this area of the brain can make behavioral changes that are so necessary to rewiring your brain and correcting eating behaviors difficult. "I am stubborn, and my brain is as stubborn as a mule—it wants to hold on to its old ways forever." This is how Jordan, who was struggling with muscular pain caused by chronic tension, as well as mood swings and overweight, expressed her dismay that her brain was taking too long to rewire itself.

Finally, there is the *pleasure arc*, brain areas that coordinate their efforts to deliver your personal network of pleasure pathways. Once wired to eating pleasure, the system gets stronger with each pleasurable meal. A strong eating pleasure network can result in powerful food urges that are as difficult to resist as cravings for addictive drugs. Table 3-1 (pages 74–76) summarizes what each of these five brain areas is and does—and why it's important in terms of eating. Take some time now to review the chart to see how your brain works to influence the way you eat.

Now, get ready to put your own brain to work. The next several pages contain statements that correspond to each of the five areas of the brain. Answer yes (sounds like me) or no (really doesn't describe me) to each statement. At the end of each set of statements, count your number of yes answers, and write the number in the appropriate box. As you can guess, what we're doing here is mapping your self-descriptions to the pertinent parts of your brain. This will help us home in on those parts that need retraining.

Of course, all your trouble spots won't be confined to any one area of your brain; each area will prompt both yes and no answers. But the proportion of affirmatives will be a guide to retraining your eating brain: the area that receives the most yes answers will be your primary target for retraining, the one with the next greatest number will be target number two, and so on. The kinds of retraining exercises we design for you also will depend on which particular part of your brain needs the most work. Obviously, it's important to be scrupulously honest and very thoughtful as you work your way through these statements. Ready? Go.

Prefrontal Cortex

	Y	N
1. I have a hard time waiting in lines.	✓	
2. When I see something I want, I have to buy it, even when I can't really afford it.	✓	
3. I rarely achieve what I set out to do.		✓
4. I am not organized.		✓
5. I have trouble paying attention.		✓
6. I find it hard to wait my turn.	✓	
7. I have trouble remembering things.		✓
8. I have a history of abusing alcohol.		✓
9. I overeat.	✓	
10. I lose focus and quickly lose interest in my weight-loss program.	✓	
11. I have trouble thinking about the consequences of my actions.		✓
12. I rarely question the motives behind my actions and feelings.		✓
13. I am easily bored.	✓	
14. I have a hard time delaying pleasure.		✓
15. I am not a restful sleeper.	✓	
16. I feel like I am in a mental fog.		✓
17. There's usually drama in my life.		✓
18. I speak in a loud tone.	✓	
19. I talk too much.		✓
20. I talk too little.		✓
21. I often put my foot in my mouth.		✓
22. I feel depressed or have been diagnosed with depression.		✓

Total number of yes answers: ___8___

Limbic System

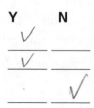

	Y	N
1. I often feel lonely.	✓	
2. It's difficult for me to trust others.	✓	
3. I find it difficult to feel close to other people.		✓

4. I have a hard time finding meaning in my life.

5. I am a worrier.

6. I either feel really active and positive, or exhausted and emotionally raw.

7. I feel irritable.

8. I frequently get tearful.

9. I overeat comfort foods.

10. I have abused alcohol and drugs.

11. I frequently feel dissatisfied.

12. I wish I were more easygoing.

13. I don't feel connected to people around me.

14. I am forgetful.

15. For me the glass is usually half empty.

16. I rarely finish what I start; I lose interest or start something else.

17. I have lower back pain.

18. I think I could be much happier than I am now.

19. I overeat and then purge.

20. I have been diagnosed with depression.

21. It's hard for me to fight my negative feelings.

22. I have trouble sleeping.

23. I don't find much joy in what others consider fun.

24. I suffer from low self-esteem.

Total number of yes answers: _____11_____

Basal Ganglia

	Y	N
1. When I am nervous, my hands and other parts of my body shake.	✓	
2. I fidget; I am restless.		✓
3. I am—or have been—bulimic.		✓

4. I find it hard to sit still for long periods of time—such as in the movies. ___ ✓

5. My neck muscles are tense. ___ ✓

6. I panic easily. ✓ ___

7. I get headaches or migraines. ___ ✓

8. I have clammy hands. ___ ✓

9. I spend a lot of time worrying about what others think of me. ✓ ___

10. I am afraid of conflict and avoid it. ✓ ___

11. I have trouble falling asleep or staying asleep. ___ ✓

12. I find it difficult to obey the speed limit when I drive. ___ ✓

13. I am an overachiever. ___ ✓

14. I overeat on weekends or during my free time. ✓ ___

15. I have high blood pressure. ___ ✓

16. At times, I feel a tightness in my chest or find it hard to breathe. ___ ✓

17. I am easily startled. ___ ✓

18. I have a "nervous stomach." ✓ ___

19. I get soreness in my shoulders and neck. ___ ✓

20. I overschedule my days, then feel worn down and spent trying to do all I've planned. ___ ✓

21. I feel self-conscious in social situations. ___ ✓

22. I like to chew—pencils, nails, crunchy foods. ___ ✓

23. I don't remember how I get minor cuts and bruises. ___ ✓

Total number of yes answers: __6__

Cingulate Gyrus

	Y	N
1. I feel pressured and jittery.		✓
2. My friends and family think I'm stubborn.		✓

3. I am a worrier. ✓
4. I like everything in its proper place.
5. I am neat.
6. I can't let go of my negative thoughts. ✓
7. I am a high achiever.
8. I don't do well on tests. ✓
9. I frequently feel worn down.
10. I don't like last-minute changes. ✓
11. I hold grudges.
12. Little things annoy me. ✓
13. It's hard to get an idea out of my mind. ✓
14. I think about food too much. ✓
15. I have abused alcohol or other drugs.
16. Once I have a plan, it's difficult to change it for others. ✓
17. I find it hard to control myself when others block my way.
18. I shop compulsively.
19. I eat compulsively. ✓
20. I am often in pain.
21. I like gambling.
22. I think of what's wrong before I consider what's right in most situations. ✓
23. I have been diagnosed with an eating disorder in the past.
24. I am rigid in my ways.
25. I wish I were more creative. ✓
26. I'm headstrong in an argument.
27. I have exhibited road rage.

Total number of yes answers: 11

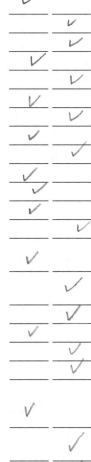

Pleasure Arc

	Y	N
1. I sense that my love for the taste of food is more than other people's.		✓

2. I use highly embellished language to describe my love for food—scrumptious, amazing, unbelievable. ✔

3. I am addicted to food. ✔

4. I relish the thought of food. ✔

5. I have abused alcohol or other drugs. ✔

6. Food is my friend. ✔

7. I like taking risks. ✔

8. I have a can of soda, gum, or a snack within reach most of the time. ✔

9. I can't wait to take a favorite food home; I will eat it en route or as soon as possible. ✔

10. Eating gives me a feeling of euphoria. ✔

11. I tend to overeat the same types of foods over and over again. ✔

12. I have strong cravings for sweets. ✔

13. I have strong cravings for high-fat foods. ✔

14. I am disorganized. ✔

15. When dieting to lose weight, I feel easily deprived. ✔

16. I tend to binge when I am under stress. ✔

17. I overeat sweet, creamy, soft foods. ✔

18. I binge for a day or more the day I go off my diet. ✔

19. I am impulsive. ✔

20. I procrastinate. ✔

21. I am an extrovert. ✔

22. I am easily distracted. ✔

23. I have purged to control my weight. ✔

24. I usually rush through my meal. ✔

25. I blow things out of proportion. ✔

Total number of yes answers: ___//___

It's both possible and likely that you will score high in more than one brain site. Such overlap is normal. But the highest score points to the area that most dominates your particular eating patterns and habits. Maybe the prefrontal cortex dominates, and your eating is driven by impulse. Or you're an "emotional eater," whose eating pattern zigzags because your limbic system dominates. Or you're simply addicted to eating pleasure in eating patterns dominated by the pleasure arc.

Whatever the result, your score is telling you which part or parts need to perform better if your brain is to find balance in healthful ways rather than by defaulting to food. That means you finally know where to focus the retraining of your brain to manage your weight successfully.

Now that you have a better idea of your vulnerable or trouble spots and can name them, you can see even more precisely how they pull your eating strings. The next step is to reframe your understanding of overeating accordingly: "I overeat because the [indicated area] in my brain is overactive. My brain has learned to use the chemicals that result from eating certain foods to calm and balance this area." Notice how this sentence immediately leads you to take corrective steps toward soothing the affected brain area—before you even begin thinking about a diet.

Once you know the degree of wobbling and the possible brain areas behind your overeating, you can dedicate special effort and time to using the tools and actions recommended in the OPT program for strengthening and stabilizing these areas.

This is the whole point of using your head to lose weight! Use your brain's own power to help it rewire itself away from unwanted eating. The OPT program teaches you the steps— effective tools that automatically lead your brain to improve.

Table 3-1

Brain Area	Function	Impact on Eating if the Area Is Unstable

Prefrontal cortex (the rational brain)	• Executive functions
	• Theoretical knowledge
	• Imagination
	• Associations
	• Abstract thinking
	• Delay of gratification
	• Planning
	• Complex cognitive operations
	• Impulse control
	• Inhibition of self-destructive impulses and behaviors
		• It's harder for you to stop eating the wrong foods.
		• It's tough for you to stay focused on your weight-loss task.
		• Eating tends to be impulsive and unplanned.
		• You find it tough to do the following:
		  Plan, anticipate
		  Persevere in the event of setbacks
		  Avoid overeating situations
		  Avoid out-of-control eating
		  Remain aware of the implications of overeating

Limbic system (the emotional brain)	• Behaviors necessary for survival—sleep, sex, sociability • Affective functions—fear, anger, passion, love, hate, joy, sadness, etc.	• You have intense cravings for high-calorie comfort foods • You overeat or undereat to overcome emotional bumps. • You feel addicted to certain foods or all food. • You are influenced by foodscape eating cues. • You can limit overeating when reminded the food is unhealthy. • You eat more healthfully when others around you eat healthfully.

- You experience feelings of depression, sadness, low self-worth, discomfort, irritability, and dissatisfaction.
- You feel detached and socially isolated, making it even harder to fight your negative feelings.
- You overeat when you feel particularly nervous and restless.
- You overeat foods you don't particularly enjoy.
- You continue to eat after a meal gets cold, or you eat food you find unappetizing.
- You eat as "something to do" or as a way of "swallowing" your feelings.
- You eat unconsciously—watching TV, driving, in a movie theater, reading, or at your desk.
- You prefer biting into crunchy foods.
- You experience symptoms of nervousness and stress—muscle tension, ticks, tremors, headaches, panic, and worry about what others think of you.
- You don't take chances or confront people; you avoid all conflict.

Basal ganglia (the tension-regulating brain)

- Suppression of unwanted actions that might interfere with a desired behavior

(continued)

Brain Area	Function	Impact on Eating if the Area Is Unstable
Cingulate gyrus (the flexibility-regulating brain)	• Adjustment of the body's responses to emotional experience • Regulation of pain response • Regulation of aggressive behavior	• You overeat the same foods over long periods of time. • You eat on a fixed schedule or by habit, regardless of hunger. • You overeat mainly to quell physical symptoms. • You have difficulty giving up old ways of cooking and eating. • You regularly crave the same food at about the same time.
Pleasure arc (the feel-good part of the brain)	• Regulation of euphoria and pleasure • Located in the midbrain, triggered by any substance that increases endorphins and dopamine and serotonin, resulting in feelings of pleasure • When underactivated, it results in the opposite of pleasure, anhedonia • Determines the sensitivity to pleasure, neurochemicals • These networks signal the need for pleasure to other systems with intense urgency which prompts them to immediate action.	• When underactive or when you lose sensitivity to its pleasurable effects, you may experience intense cravings, especially for densely caloric foods that you can rarely control. • You respond with intense pleasure to highly caloric foods, getting the "high" usually associated with highly addictive drugs. • By chronically overeating densely caloric foods you can cause this system to block release of pleasurable neurochemicals normally obtained through eating, leaving you constantly searching for more and more comfort foods. • Your powerful cravings may be best addressed with methods used to treat alcohol and drug addictions.

4

What the Eating Brain Has Done, It Can Undo

The Ever-Changing Brain

Neuroplasticity is the brain's lifelong ability to reorganize and restructure itself as a result of experience. Specifically, it means that as you change or acquire new skills such as developing new eating behaviors, your brain will physically alter to reflect those changes. As you can imagine, the process has its pluses and minuses.

That the brain is capable of change is not surprising. As an organ, its main function is to help us adapt to the world around us, and as the world around us changes, the brain shifts activity from one location to another and changes its actual structure—the very functions it performs. The environment's demands determine what is kept and what is eliminated.

The brain provides the raw material, but the environment is the sculptor. For example, our modern brain retains only a fraction of the capabilities for visual processing and smell that our primitive ancestors had. This is because we no longer rely as heavily on smell or acute vision for survival. On the other hand, the amount of brain tissue dedicated to processing cognitive information has grown dramatically because that's what today's environment requires. The brain makes adaptive changes to accommodate our critical needs.

The process begins very early on, even before birth. Indeed, from the moment you started flexing your fist in the womb, your interaction with the world affected your brain's development. Your mother's health, gestational hormones, the circumstances of your birth, and later the speed and consistency with which someone came to you when you cried as an infant—these and other experiences influenced how your brain began to thrive and grow or how it became wobbly and imbalanced.

Today, through imaging techniques and other technologies, we can see inside the brain so minutely that we can pinpoint the changes effected by these different experiences. Moreover, we can actually identify the specific changes they triggered in enzymes or proteins. Often, these changes can be correlated with behavior, including eating.

Such studies have shown, for example, that if a baby's cry is ignored consistently enough, the structures inside the limbic system, the emotional center of the brain, are eventually altered. The brain's communication pathways are literally weakened, and there is a reduction in the volume of chemicals the brain releases. These microscopic changes lead to larger structural changes that can later result in such problems as anxiety, depression, and overeating.

You might be wondering how an organ that's evolved with the single purpose of helping us thrive in whatever world we're born into can make changes in our wiring that can sabotage us in the long term. The brain is not callous; it simply makes adaptive changes. When the baby's cries are ignored, her brain decides there is no point wasting energy in keeping the area involved in crying active. It's better to shift attention and energy to other functions, maybe areas that help the infant make eye contact or raise her arms high. The brain has to find another way to ensure that the baby gets the attention she needs to survive but can't afford to preserve what it thinks is useless.

This ability to be altered (plasticity) is the brain's most essential feature. Without it, we could not learn, develop, or progress. The other side of the coin, as we saw in Chapter 2 when we talked about the cause of your wobble, is that the brain can react to rapid or repeated changes in the environment in ways that turn out to be harmful. That's exactly what has happened with eating.

Simply put, our contemporary foodscape has morphed too rapidly for the brain to adapt as carefully as it could otherwise. I liken it to thousands of memos coming into an office at once, each one decreeing a slight change in procedure. How could you keep up with the new policies without becoming overwhelmed or confused? You couldn't. All you could really retain is the gist of what the new policies might be.

> Rapid changes in food abundance have not led to corresponding changes in the eating brain. It still operates under the now-obsolete principles of the more food, the better and the more caloric the food, the better.

Similarly, rapid changes in food abundance have not led to corresponding changes in the eating brain. It still operates under the now-obsolete principles of the more food, the better and the more caloric the food, the better. Rapid changes have caught the eating brain off guard. As a result, we are operating without the required checks and balances needed to stay healthy in today's world.

The Moth, the Flame, and the Eating Brain

It's a bit like the moth drawn to a light. The moth appears to us to be heading deliberately toward self-immolation. Is this an evolutionary mistake? Don't all creatures seek to survive, thrive, and pass on their genes through procreation? Yes, but the moth's evolution seems to be caught in a bit of a time lag. Millions of years ago, before artificial light existed, the moth evolved mechanisms to orient itself using existing light from the sun and stars. Had artificial lights played a role in moth evolution, moths today would presumably have mechanisms to distinguish between artificial and natural light, and those moths that made the distinction successfully would have been naturally selected to survive and thrive. Who knows? Perhaps that evolutionary transition is taking place now, and moths in another million years will be able to distinguish easily between the lights that guide them and the lights that may destroy them.

Similarly, the human brain evolved its balance regulation and craving for food during a time that far predates the contemporary foodscape. There was no more need for mechanisms to curb overeating than for moths to distinguish artificial from celestial light. Like those ill-fated moths, humans do not really mean to do themselves in; they are just carrying out instructions that at one time boosted their chances of survival.

What all this comes down to is that you're up against some pretty powerful forces when you attempt to lose weight by changing the way you eat. You're not just battling your own willpower, and you're not just confronting a foodscape that constantly invites you to eat unhealthy foods. No, you're actually pitting yourself against your brain, a brain that is inherently poised toward weight gain. What's more, that inherent predisposition toward weight gain is exacerbated by two important realities. One is that the brain has few protective mechanisms against the foodscape's abundance of high-calorie foods luring you to eat.

The brain hasn't been able to keep up, in the evolutionary sense, with all the rapid changes in food abundance in our era. It still operates under the defunct theory that the more food there is, the better. Seek and eat as much as possible and store the extra calories; that's the naturally selected path to survival—or was two million years ago. Today's brain, still reading that first survival memo, has simply been caught off guard, and as a result, we are operating without the required checks and balances needed to stay healthy in today's world.

The other reality is the insidious targeting of this vulnerability—the sparsity of checks and balances to regulate eating—by food marketers. In a very real sense, the brain's natural tendencies collide with modern neuromarketing, the kind of marketing so rampant in the contemporary foodscape, that makes use of neuroscientific data to manipulate our brains to buy and eat certain foods in big portions.

The good news is that we're going to make use of the neuroplasticity that is so central to the brain's genius to counter these realities. The changes in your eating behavior can rewrite your old program, and the hardwiring that ran the old unhealthy eating behaviors can be restructured. In this chapter, you'll learn what makes the brain thrive so that it turns away from your wobble and toward healthy eating. You'll also learn about those environmental factors that can make the brain unsteady and must be avoided if you're going to manage your weight healthfully for life.

Can You Change Your Brain? Yes!

Research shows pretty clearly that changing the brain through retraining works. For one thing, the concept of cognitive rehabilitation has been shown to work on stroke victims and even among the elderly who have begun to experience so-called senior moments. In essence, the brain's activity is simply rerouted from damaged or eroding brain tissue to the remaining healthy tissue, helping it grow new connections and strengthen those already spared.

How does this work? For many decades, it was assumed that nerve cells or neurons damaged from head trauma, stroke, or Alzheimer's were basically dead and gone, that these neurons were the only cells in the body that could not be regenerated. This rather dogmatic wisdom was turned upside down when neuroscientists, key among them Elizabeth Gould, discovered that animals exposed to stimulating home cages—"decorated" in a variety of colors and toys—actually experienced nerve cell regeneration. The brain simply grew new cells and became healthier and fitter, specifically through the growth of neuronal processes in the cortex and the proliferation of glial cells, which support and nourish the nervous system. Shortly after this discovery, the 1990s were declared the "decade of the brain," by George H. W. Bush as advanced imaging technology allowed us to peek into living human brains, which is why history is being made in this area even as you read this.

> For many decades, it was assumed that nerve cells or neurons damaged from head trauma, stroke, or Alzheimer's were basically dead and gone, that these neurons were the only cells in the body that could not be regenerated.

Dr. Gould's findings were replicated by other scientists and have had profound consequences in the arena of neurological treatment methods. But that was only the beginning; the scientific and health communities are making further discoveries all the time. In a nutshell, these discoveries show that in addition to colors and toys, a walk in the woods, certain foods, and certain medications are what is called *neurotrophic*—literally, "nourishing to nerve cells." Neurotrophic substances and conditions help nurture existing cells and increase production of the protein cells needed to survive and perform well.

Certainly, if the brain can come back from damage and erosion from a stroke, it can also come back from the "damage" of inappropriate eating habits. That's what the Gould research tells us. What you'll do in the OPT program is make use of this research to change your own brain. You'll use your brain's intrinsic wiring to coax it to do the right thing and eat healthfully.

Certainly, if the brain can come back from damage and erosion from a stroke, it can also come back from the "damage" of inappropriate eating habits.

Lifestyle Changes the Brain

But how? To answer this, let's look at the study conducted for the Healthy Longevity Program (Gary Small, *The Longevity Bible* [New York: Hyperion, 2006]). For fourteen days, half of the study's participants simply carried out their normal everyday activities, while the other half were required to follow these daily routines:

- A walk
- Mental exercises such as puzzles and brain teasers
- A diet of foods high in omega-3 fatty acids and antioxidants and low in glycemic index
- Relaxation techniques for stress reduction

At the end of the fourteen days, the participants on the longevity program showed improvement in working memory and other brain fitness measures relative to those who did nothing. A sophisticated PET scan, which enables deep brain observation, compared the "before" and "after" brain activity of those who went through the program and those who did not. The brains of program participants registered greater activity in the dorsal lateral prefrontal cortex—the area roughly above the end of the eyebrow—an area of the brain associated with working memory.

Bottom line? If the work of Gould and other neuroscientists proved that the brain can "come back" and rewire itself—that we can undo the damage of even a lifetime of unhealthy and inappropriate eating—the healthy longevity study shows that the rewiring can happen pretty quickly even with relatively simple lifestyle changes.

Become Your Brain's Personal Neurotrainer

The conclusion is inescapable that with appropriate changes in your environment and lifestyle, you can change your brain— and thus, the way you eat. Instead of using food to balance itself, your brain will look to forces and factors that make it thrive to find its equilibrium. First, let's talk about what to avoid so that your brain doesn't become weaker and unstable.

> The conclusion is inescapable that with appropriate changes in your environment and lifestyle, you can change your brain— and thus, the way you eat.

Seven Things to Avoid

Obviously, a lack of any of the neurotrophic factors can hinder brain fitness. But seven other factors that adversely affect the brain's ability to thrive and renew itself should be noted. For the most part, these factors reflect inadequate physical, social, and emotional interaction, often starting back in childhood. With this type of neurological insufficiency, some key experiences in life such as love, joy, empathy, active interest, curiosity, and even healthy attachment to another person may be beyond our ability. It's simple, if sad: if key pieces of the hardware are missing, it will show up in our behavior.

- A Brain-Harming Diet
- Not Enough Pleasure
- A Lack of Physical Activity
- Emotional Disorders and Physical Illness
- Stress
- Premature Aging
- Preventable Hardships of Poverty

So here are seven "antineurotrophic" factors to try to avoid in more detail.

A Brain-Harming Diet Yes, a diet rich in particular nutrients was the first factor mentioned among the top twenty to embrace as part of your environment. But it is equally important to avoid certain foods and eating patterns if you are going to keep your brain healthy—and help it keep you healthy. Specifically, try to avoid high-fat foods, high-calorie foods, and manufactured foods.

Highly caloric, low-fiber foods and foods that are high in fats, particularly animal fats, can cause increased inflammation in the body—a process that generates free radicals and leads to damage of all body tissues, particularly brain tissue. Eating a diet high in animal fats can also harm the brain in another way: it results in inflammation that weakens the walls of blood vessels, which leads to thickening of the arteries. Blocked or partially blocked arteries mean less oxygen and nutrients reaching the brain. Since the brain is the most oxygen-sensitive organ in the body, even small decreases in blood flow affect its function.

High-calorie foods are best thought of as potent drugs. They release their ingredients inside the gastrointestinal tract (also known as the primitive brain, since it stems from the same neo-natal structure as the brain, the neural tube). Once ingested, these foods—fats, sugar, chocolate, and the like—can trigger the release of gastrointestinal as well as brain chemicals and hor-mones that disrupt the health and normal function of our genetic potential. Remember, findings from the field of nutrigenomics tell us that foods can change our basic DNA building blocks.

In my view, the biggest threat to our well-being by unhealthy overeating is to our cognition. Thinking, learning, planning, and problem solving and the speed at which we figure things out appear to be slower in obese adults and obese children. Unhealthy overeating affects brain chemicals and hormones that disrupt our attention and therefore interfere with our awareness of the world around us, dull our senses, and create the "dirty windshield effect." In other words, the release and regulation of neurotransmitters directly affect the intensity and duration of your attention and ability to intake and process information; interfering with those cognitive abilities causes a lack of clarity and cloudiness of sensory input. You might say that high-calorie foods are good for something after all: they buffer you from the full-blown effects of anything unpleasant. As your brain's neu-rotrainer, your first job is to stay mindful that if the world around you is creating more discomfort than you can handle, your brain may opt for the slight sedation brought by these foods.

High-calorie foods are also marked by a high glycemic index; they raise blood sugar levels the instant they reach your stom-ach. While this "rush" can deliver a powerful punch of satisfac-tion, it files that reaction in the addiction segment of your brain rather than in the nourishment section. Later, when activated, this brain area can generate intense cravings that are as hard to resist as the old demons of nicotine, alcohol, and other physi-ologically addictive drugs.

In general, avoid manufactured foods, especially those that are so filled with preservatives and synthetic additives that they have a long shelf life. Food ingredients like HFCS and palm oil may affect the cardiovascular system which, in addition to harming the rest of your body, also lower the blood supply and oxygen to the brain. This can reduce the brain's ability to regenerate neurons or maintain healthy strong networks, which may in turn lead to diminished mental alertness and "sluggishness" of intellect.

In addition to avoiding these particular foods, avoid overeating in general. Too much of even a good thing—that is, healthy foods—is too much. Overeating burdens your body, which has to work extra hard to digest, absorb, and eliminate waste products. This work takes away from finite energy supplies that could be used for more constructive things like being curious and playful—two attributes that help the brain thrive. We also now know that diseases like cancer, as well as the debilitating effects of aging, are accelerated by the overconsumption of any food.

Not Enough Pleasure More and more Americans seem to suffer from anhedonia, or chronically diminished sense of pleasure. The fact that more and more of us are lacking in pleasure and satisfaction in the midst of economic prosperity is puzzling. However, studies have shown that having more money than needed to satisfy your basic needs, doesn't buy happiness. That is, income is correlated with happiness only when it's too short of a supply to meet basic needs. Beyond that level it ceases to be predictive of or correlate with parameters of happiness like pleasure and satisfaction.

Anhedonia could be partly the result of living an increasingly isolated, lonely life. A recent study found a decrease in the number of friends Americans talk to on a consistent basis.

Fewer friends means less social support, an essential ingredient for pleasure and well being.

A Lack of Physical Activity An inactive lifestyle shrinks and atrophies muscles you can see, as in your arms and abdomen. It also shrinks a hidden muscle—the brain. Physical inactivity can contribute to smaller neural networks, both the shrinking of existing networks and the failure of new cells to attach to existing networks, probably due to the negative effects on the cardiovascular system that compromise oxygen supply and through brain tissue damage from inflammation. In addition, a sedentary life makes less use of brain systems that orient us in space—that is, that keep us from getting lost or losing track of our keys. You know the rule: if you don't use these brain areas, your brain assumes you don't need them, so it doesn't waste energy fortifying and maintaining them. The result can be getting lost while driving, losing your coordination, even losing your place in a conversation. I bet you hadn't realized that being a couch potato can have such wide-ranging unpleasant consequences!

Contrary to what you may expect, the brain thrives not when on vacation or on the weekend, but when engaged comfortably and fully on achieving a goal. In fact, it appears that when you go on vacation, so does your brain. "Vacation brain" can mean a drop of as many as twenty IQ points.

Emotional Disorders and Physical Illness Optimal brain health is certainly compromised by conditions we cannot always avoid. Alzheimer's, muscular sclerosis, autism, mood disorders like depression or anxiety, and thought disorders like schizophrenia can inhibit the brain's optimal function. Anything you can do to treat, mitigate, or retard the effects of these disorders will benefit your brain.

Stress Arguably the most neurotoxic chemical soup that the brain is routinely exposed to is manufactured inside our own bodies every time we feel overextended or under stress. The soup is made up of neurochemicals and hormones such as cortisol and adrenaline, both of which are damaging to brain tissue and just about every other body part. Stress-triggered chemicals like epinephrine constrict the blood vessels; over time, this can mean that a reduced supply of oxygenated blood is reaching your body's main organs. Stress releases free radicals that damage tissue and increase appetite as well as increasing fat deposition, especially around the abdomen.

The emotional rawness that stress produces, a reflection of a red-hot limbic system, causes us to seek soothing calm in foods, especially comfort foods that tend to be high in calories. We've seen in studies of adults who suffered childhood abuse or trauma how the shock and pain of these experiences harmed some of the brain's key structures. Like a number of Vietnam veterans, these victims of violence show a significantly smaller hippocampus, the area of the brain associated with emotional memories. Extreme stresses damage the limbic system (the emotional brain) and set the stage for anxiety, depression, rage, and unhappiness that can last a lifetime.

But you don't have to suffer abuse or go to war to respond in this way. Any form of stress can leave the brain in a state of distress with unmet needs. The result? The brain will substitute one limbic need for another by using food to quell anger or to bring relaxation and safety. Call it "limbic relief." Weight gain is almost inevitable.

Premature Aging It's absolutely unavoidable, but the brain loses about 9 percent of its original mass as it ages—a loss that is more pronounced in men than in women—and that affects thinking, memory, and planning. It just happens. Only by slowing the effects of aging through helping our brains thrive can we retard this process; we will almost surely not put a stop to it.

Poverty Poverty and factors that typically result, such as poor housing, violence, overcrowding, lack of positive stimulation, and a grim, often barren environment, are the highest risks to brain health. Each of these factors acting alone can devastate the ability of the brain to thrive, but poverty typically combines several if not all of them, making it an even stronger anti-neurotrophic factor. Adding to the risk of developing diseases is the physical and emotional stress caused by discrimination and social disapproval. In short, a bleak world doesn't entice or motivate the body as a whole—or the brain in particular—to thrive. But the picture is not completely hopeless: the negative strikes brought on by poverty can be blocked by a single key supportive relationship, such as with a mother. Remember, you can find yourself living in poverty and still manage to avoid some of the aftermath to your brain.

More factors are bound to be identified, but these seven are key triggers that cause the brain to lose its vitality, richness, and balance. They make it wobble and subsequently turn to eating as a means of compensation.

Your Brain-Boosting Environment

Create an environment filled with these top neurotrophics:

- A Brain-Boosting Diet
- Flexibility
- Idle Time
- Challenge and Industry
- Positive Social Interaction
- Exercise

- Beauty
- Touch
- Novelty
- Sleep
- Practice

"Feed" your brain on these experiences, and soon you'll be well on your way toward retraining your brain to thrive on healthy eating patterns.

A Brain-Healthy Diet We've long known that "you are what you eat." As it turns out, that's especially true for the brain. So you won't be surprised to learn that all the foods we know to be good for us are very effective in helping the brain thrive. Rule of thumb? Anything heart-smart is brain-smart. Improved cardiovascular health lets the brain receive unhindered oxygen and glucose for mental processing. So Mediterranean- and Japanese-style cuisines help the brain flourish. Antioxidants are also key; they lessen the formation of free radicals that can damage organs and blood vessels. Since the brain is the heaviest user of the body's energy, it is particularly vulnerable to free-radical damage. Brain tissue is sensitive to inflammation, so foods rich in omega-3 fatty acids, such as fish and leafy green vegetables, are also important. A low-calorie, low-fat diet with limited amounts of simple carbohydrates can slow the effects of aging. Fruits, vegetables, whole grains, nuts—all the foods we know are good for the body are also good for the brain. Chapter 7 will provide you with more details about eating well for better brain health.

Flexibility The brain responds well to finding new and different ways of going about things as opposed to rigid and restrained methods. We have known for years that rigid personalities are not as successful in problem solving or maintaining mental health, and now we've learned that even microscopic organisms have a greater chance of advancing and developing when their physical appearance is flexible and constantly open to change. The lesson? Preserve some order, but stay loose and make sure you're willing to accept and embrace changes in your life; it's good for the brain.

Idle Time It has been said that we stumble on the most creative thinking while we are in three places beginning with the letter b: bus, bathtub, and bed. Changing context and "idling" activates different parts of the brain and helps direct its activity to areas not usually frequented. The electrical brainwave activity patterns shift, and more often than not, infrequently used brain areas and novel brainwave patterns have the answers we are looking for and help shift our perspective.

Challenge and Industry Contrary to conventional wisdom, we are not happier on weekends or on vacation. We are more likely to feel "in flow," or fully present, while engaged in a task in which we can lose ourselves and that we find at once enjoyable and challenging. Behind the experience of flow is an incredible soup of neurochemicals and brain activity that produces key emotional memories, learning, pleasure, and calm attention. Being in flow alters consciousness. We become fully engrossed in the project at hand. Time stands still. It usually happens when we do something we find difficult but still within the range of our capabilities. If a task is too difficult, the resulting frustration will keep us from feeling completely involved. Significantly, a key characteristic of healthy centenarians is being physically and mentally active beyond their sixties.

From crosswords and Sudoku to learning a musical instrument or a new language, challenge builds brain mass, space, and connections. Challenging the brains of people with neurological conditions such as Alzheimer's has been shown to slow the progress of the disease and reduce cognitive decline. One easy way to provide a stimulating challenge is to inhibit your normal tendencies. If you're right-handed, force yourself to use your left hand for as many everyday activities as you can—emptying the dishwasher, turning the pages of your book, working the TV remote. Living in an environment that is physically and mentally stimulating not only helps maintain brain health, but also protects the brain from the deterioration that results from aging and neurological conditions.

Positive Social Interaction Numerous studies show that the more positive social encounters or social support we have, the happier and healthier we are. The reason? Such interaction promotes the feel-good chemicals that affirm a positive sense of self and make us feel accepted, secure, and confident. Even a simple "good morning" from a passing stranger can improve mood for hours, while strong support networks—family and friends—have been shown to boost the immune system.

You've probably heard of "laugh therapy," in which therapists attempt to inject some humor into life's situations. You may have even heard of the benefits of "laughing yoga" to the body and soul. Whether it's a roar over a good joke or casual, easy laughter from a pleasant interaction, the emotional response comes from the limbic system and neocortex—the emotional brain and the area responsible for higher mental function, respectively—and helps the whole brain thrive. Laughter is indeed the best medicine for everything, and it's free. Remember this: it is the teller of a joke, not the listener, who laughs the most, so take the floor and tell a joke.

Volunteering, exhibiting kindness, or simply helping out friends and family is another great way to boost your brain health. Extending a helping hand does as much for the giver as it does for the recipient. It raises the levels of dopamine, serotonin, and a cascade of subsequent happy chemicals that elevate your mood and emotional state. Talk about a gift that keeps on giving! You can start your own mass movement of global brain fitness with a single, public act of kindness.

Exercise Exercise helps the brain maintain its muscle mass and build more muscle. It increases the blood flow to the brain, activates the areas involved in memory (the hippocampus), coordination (the cerebellum), and stress (the locus coeruleus). Exercise can even reverse age-related degeneration, no matter how old you are; in lab tests, the brains of older animals who exercised regenerated up to 50 percent more new cells than those of younger inactive animals.

Beauty Beauty bathes the brain with trophic chemicals; you feel better in the short term even as these chemicals help rewire your brain for the long term. Beauty has a positive effect on cognitive function, improving your ability to solve problems and sharpening sensory experiences. These neurochemicals also affect the quality of your emotions, filling you with optimism, well-being, and a positive regard for yourself and others.

Beauty that is visually stimulating is particularly helpful. Recent advances have enabled scientists to observe changes inside single visual cells by inserting an imaging system inside the brains of living animals. When animals are housed in an enriched environment—one that is visually stimulating and contains an abundance of textures—scientists can observe nerve cells changing in response to these enrichments. Specifically, visual enrichment triggered release of a protein that enhanced the quality of incoming visual information. Visual enrichment makes you see things more sharply and guides which areas you look at, helping you become an even more efficient detector and evaluator of the world around you. In terms of the brain, a visually enriching environment is one that is complex: it contains corners, angles, contours and contrasts; in other words images that are loaded with the most information. It's further confirmation that neurons have plasticity; they respond to what you see. By actively designing your world with that in mind, you can help sharpen and develop your brain.

Touch Touch is healing and stimulating. Massage has been shown not only to relax muscles, but also to increase the levels of dopamine and serotonin, neurotranmitters that carry messages and signals of mood elevation between cells. It isn't even necessary to be emotionally invested in the person touching you to gain positive effects; any form of being touched—willingly, of course—triggers neurotrophic chemicals and responses in the limbic system. The more touching, the greater the number of cells generated inside the amygdala and the richer and more rewarding the experience.

Novelty We know that infants as well as adults prefer novel images to familiar ones. But why should we seek out unfamiliar experiences? It turns out that novelty triggers a specific loop inside the brain that enhances learning, so we retain more information and are motivated to explore the world and learn even more.

Sleep Getting enough sleep on a regular basis is necessary for your brain to flourish. Sleepless nights mean cranky days, and we tend to soothe crankiness by nibbling. Sleeplessness causes low levels of leptin, a protein hormone that regulates energy intake. Low leptin makes you cranky, and that raises your level of ghrelin, the "hunger hormone" that stimulates your appetite and makes you eat.

Unlike other sleep disorders, the kinds of sleep shortages that drive overeating appear to be directly related to daily stress. That's why the strategy for sleeping soundly in order to achieve weight loss focuses on minimizing stress throughout the day.

High-calorie foods are another serious culprit in this equation. Accumulating data show that eating such foods more or less chronically causes the brain to lose its ability to regulate functions like sleep and emotion as well as weight. The reason seems to be that the foods trigger a brain malfunction when it comes to integrating information. A host of physical, cognitive, and emotional syndromes results—a global dysregulation that is evident in excess weight, cognitive deficits, sleep disorders, and emotional problems.

So once again, what makes the brain strong—its dynamic nature—also proves to be its Achilles heel: when one system is performing suboptimally, the failure can cascade to other systems and impair their performance. For the most part, the kinds of sleep disturbances the overweight suffer are stress-related, so by targeting your stress, you improve your chances of successful weight loss and weight management—and of course, you will also sleep more soundly.

Practice The old adage rings true: practice does make perfect, especially if you practice perfectly. Do you know why? Each time you practice a skill, from kicking a soccer ball to playing scales on the piano, the brain connections in charge of these skills get stronger. Cells move closer together, narrowing the gap or synapse between them, which helps improve performance and speed accuracy. In addition, with every repetition, the signal to generate more of this type of cell gets stronger. As a result, more cells are built. The brain may even recruit cells from neighboring areas that normally have little to do with soccer or piano playing, and enlist them to help with dribbling or playing chords, giving those functions greater neural weight and thus greater ability. Think about it: if you repeat actions that cause you to seek satisfaction from eating certain foods, your performance in this will also get stronger. The more you reinforce all of the healthy behaviors you've read about in this chapter, the stronger your brain will be and the more susceptible to the tools you'll learn to use in Chapter 6.

Bottom line? Build your environment as much as possible out of the building blocks of the neurotrophic factors; avoid as best you can the seven antineurotrophics. Keep your brain healthy so it doesn't turn to food as a solution to its imbalances. As you can see, the dynamic approach curbs eating through your brain, not mouth!

Boosting the Brain to Overcome Unhealthy Eating

Now you've seen how brain behavior is mirrored in personal behavior. People under stress from financial worries, family problems, or personal setbacks typically drop their standards of hygiene, stop wearing seat belts when they drive, and eat whatever is available at the time. People unhappy with their lives tend to give up on the luxuries of self-maintenance; they just want to survive their unhappiness. And people overwhelmed by the priorities of modern life discover that if something has to go, it's going to be health. When you are working two jobs, there is no time for a daily jog—not to mention a restful night's sleep or the classic balanced meal three times a day.

Of course, it is precisely during those times of stress or unhappiness or feeling overwhelmed that the brain, stumped for solutions to emotional and physical problems, turns to the old standby—the feeding mode. When your interactions with the world are not meeting your needs and your brain can't integrate all aspects of your life experiences to allow you to feel pleasant and comfortable, you turn to eating instead. Food becomes a tool for equilibrium; it brings balance. So what if it's a temporary solution? As scientist/author/philosopher Rudy Rucker has said, life is, after all, one temporary solution after another.

> It is precisely during those times of stress or unhappiness or feeling overwhelmed that the brain, stumped for solutions to emotional and physical problems, turns to the old standby—the feeding mode.

Your Eating Brain Revisited

Your life history—how well you have been able to meet your needs for belonging, love, industry, acceptance, and security—has shaped the connections among neurons that create the networks that make up your eating brain. These connections are translated into energy, and the pattern of this energy flow determines your individual eating pattern.

Let's take a look at how energy can be redirected toward eating. Ashley is twelve and is being raised in a loud and chaotic household. The daily drama is just too much for her empathic, quiet, and reserved nature. She is intensely angry, feeling fed up and trapped in the spectator role because she doesn't have what it takes to express herself. So she retreats to her computer and takes her snacks with her.

In Ashley's case, her inherent avoidance of conflict and aversion to loudness has led to overactivity in her limbic system: anger, sadness, vigilance, helplessness, and uncertainty. Because there were no avoidable steps that Ashley could have taken to escape her problem, her brain in its own inherent wisdom, dealt with this discomfort by overeating. The brain did a "cost-benefit analysis" and found that leaving Ashley in daily turmoil was too uncomfortable; eating offered an easy route to pleasure and escape.

As you are examining your own eating triggers, consider this. Your eating brain was wired to escape from strife and pleasure at a time in your life when you perhaps had no other plausible solutions or options; your brain deemed eating the best solution given the circumstances. This resulted in heavy use of the feeding mode. This neurobiological pathway is carved in something stronger than stone—it's carved in brain tissue. That means dieting and willpower alone really have little chance of bringing about weight loss.

Thanks to neuroplasticity, the heavy demand and use of the networks connecting eating to emotional discomfort become larger and stronger over time to the point where it takes very little in the way of frustration to catapult you into feeding mode. This hair-trigger eating response to any emotional setback or discomfort can only be resolved by reprogramming and rerouting. Your own actions, the healthier living and eating behaviors that you will be following, will help restructure your brain once again. You can put neuroplasticity to work for you.

Starting Over

The ability to move in any direction you choose at a future time appears to be at the very core of both all human nature and your individual nature. It's called starting over. When scientists examine the foundations of human nature down to the smallest particles that make up our bodies, they find that these particles start over constantly. In fact, they change direction so rapidly that scientists can't even predict their next move; the particles themselves determine the outcome of their future behavior.

Starting over is your inherent asset. Even if you grew up neglected, even if your brain has been deprived of the opportunity to flourish, even if you have been eating high-calorie foods for years, you are at this very moment in a position to determine the direction of your life.

Which direction will it be? Are you heading for a soda and nacho refill? No matter what your past experience, you don't have to. But if you want to live and eat differently from the way you are living and eating today, you first need to change your brain's electrical and neurochemical patterns. It is within your power to do that.

> Even if you grew up neglected, even if your brain has been deprived of the opportunity to flourish, even if you have been eating high-calorie foods for years, you are at this very moment in a position to determine the direction of your life.

Being open to change is essential. Rudy Rucker calls it "gnarliness"—that is, being open and amenable to change and adaptations that will help you thrive. The gnarly individual is not stuck in one brain gear, or frequency, that repeatedly drives the same eating behaviors over and over again. Instead, the gnarly brain has a smooth, well-lubricated transmission that shifts easily, depending on what is going on both inside and out.

That's the brain that will help you access and navigate the healthy universe that is just as real as—maybe even more real than—the unhealthy universe you're stuck in. The brain you retrain to fitness will reject yesterday's fast-food lunch that you ate without ever getting out of your car. Instead, it will find the balance it seeks by telling you to walk to the nearby deli on your lunch hour and order a turkey sandwich on whole-grain bread—hold the chips—before you walk back to work. Now, let's begin your brain fitness regime!

PART 3

Retrain

The Third Step

Retraining with Global Mind Fitness Tools

Would you consider biking a hundred miles in a day without proper training? Unless you are already an elite athlete, you would probably first enter a fitness training program that would gradually prepare you for the race ahead. And like any athlete—indeed, like anyone preparing for physical activity—you would begin your athletic conditioning by first focusing on overall fitness. That means paying close attention to nutrition, sleep, and overall strength training.

A naive athlete may focus on doing squats to strengthen leg muscles or timed workouts that focus on improving cycling speeds and neglect to invest time and effort to build overall physical fitness. Strong legs, though vital for biking a great distance, can hardly carry you through to the finish if the rest of your body is flabby and weak. Savvy athletes know they have to tighten their muscles and strengthen their bones first, before moving on to the conditioning specific to their sport. They know that not only is it a waste of energy to try to push a body that's not ready to be pushed, it can actually be harmful, leading to strains, sprains, and other kinds of stress injuries that can leave them laid up for months, missing the biking season altogether.

The same is true of the brain. The eating tools you will learn to use work much more efficiently and effectively on a brain that is toned, nimble, and dynamic. The twelve regulation tools, or actions, you'll start practicing in this chapter are the brain's equivalent of an overall body workout, aimed at building up your brain's strength, agility, and suppleness. They energize and augment your ability for self-regulation. They're the base on which you will later work to strengthen specific eating-related brain muscles—for example, the brain muscle that helps you choose a snack of carrots, not cake.

How Brain Boosting Works

Neurodynamics is one of the newest disciplines in neurobiology. It's a dynamic, "nonlinear" way of looking at brain function—focusing on the complex, dynamic interaction between all brain areas to explain behavior. For example, a neurodynamic model considers the combined influence of multiple mechanisms on eating behavior. A linear way of looking at eating behavior is to study changes only in brain areas that are directly involved with eating and neglect looking at the way those changes combine to cause overeating.

In the first two chapters, you learned that above all else, the brain functions as a dynamic whole—greater, more complex, and more capable—than the sum of its parts. In the case of eating behavior, scientific studies have identified inherent brain tendencies

> The twelve regulation tools, or actions, you'll start practicing in this chapter are the brain's equivalent of an overall body workout, aimed at building up your brain's strength, agility, and suppleness.

that work alone or in combination with other mechanisms to drive overeating in dynamic ways. Whenever possible, tools have been forged from scientific studies to help redirect those tendencies so as to curb eating. The brain-boosting tools that comprise the OPT program are mostly derived from this innovative discipline. For this reason, you may find it hard to see how improvements in some brain areas, let's say balance and coordination, can lead to changes in eating; at face value, they appear unrelated, but neurodynamically, they are very much interconnected.

Use these tools consciously and consistently as part of the OPT program to stimulate and nurture your brain, and your brain will stimulate and nurture you. It will find the pleasures inherent in living without resorting to food for comfort or escape.

These actions require no great effort or expense, yet they are capable of bringing profound positive results in a reasonably short time. A recent study showed that even minor lifestyle adjustments—similar to those in the OPT program—made over fourteen days resulted in measurable structural and behavioral changes in the brain as well as measurable weight loss. Subjects' brains gained efficiency, dynamism, memory capability, and function. Subsequent brain scans helped to verify these effects and identify the specific areas that were strengthened as a result of the changes.

> You may find it surprising that simple changes in lifestyle can have such profound effects on the brain and wellness.

You may find it surprising that simple changes in lifestyle can have such profound effects on the brain and wellness. We have come to expect that something as important as the brain requires extraordinary measures and technologically complex solutions for any improvement to its potential—and our behavior. But that's not so. The strong message that comes to us from a host of brain fitness literature tells us that the opposite is actually true: *the brain responds to small but consistent changes.*

The brain fitness race is won not with gimmicks, but with common sense based on science. That's what the OPT program provides, and that's why retraining the eating brain makes weight loss an achievable goal.

Two Categories of Activities

The OPT program makes use of two categories of activities to retrain your eating brain. As their names imply, one category provides an overall fitness workout for your whole brain, while the other focuses on your eating brain:

- Global Mind Fitness tools are designed to boost the brain's overall performance.
- Eating neuroregulation activities are designed specifically to decrease overeating.

Obviously, by using both sets of activities, you enhance the effectiveness of each, creating powerful counterforces to your eating urges.

The activities work by both reprogramming and rerouting your brain's neurodynamic function. Reprogramming helps you anticipate and forestall scenarios that cause you to overeat by regulating and balancing your brain, making it more powerful and dynamic—as nature intended. Rerouting distracts you from overeating pitfalls. It tries to beat your brain at its own game. If the brain focuses on a chocolate éclair, rerouting changes the focus to that woman jogging outside; she is thin, moving easily, and having a wonderful time—or so your rerouted brain tells you.

In a very real sense, this retraining enables you to manipulate your brain's weaknesses to your advantage for weight loss and many other problem areas of your life. It's how you'll ease yourself into the elusive fit universe, where healthy eating is what comes naturally.

You'll start learning the specifics of the eating activities in the next chapter. For now, let's look at some ways to ready yourself for retraining your brain and then move on to the regulation tools.

Setting a Training Schedule

Twelve steps are geared to help retrain your brain and become more balanced. It's best that you use "a-step-a-day" approach: dedicate a day to become familiar with each step or action. Take the whole day to learn how the specific action can fit into your lifestyle. Keep on adding days and actions in a cumulative way so by the end of twelve days you have incorporated all the actions. Some of these steps call on you to make specific changes to your environment and daily schedule, such as getting fit or feeding your mind. Some are attitude or mood regulators, like the mood-induction procedures, that require only a small investment of time to become part of your life. And some, such as putting on the brain brake, are brain-booster techniques you'll need to practice repeatedly. Each action is derived from proven scientific facts, and those facts are fully explained.

You will practice using a new step each day for the next twelve days. Some of these steps specifically target the part of your eating brain that needs the most help—your prefrontal cortex, limbic system, basal ganglia, cingulate gyrus, or pleasure arc. Determine the tools that target the part of your eating brain that is causing your wobble; revisit and practice them as frequently as possible.

Boosting your brain boosts your attention, your emotions, and your ability to solve problems.

Really dedicate one day to each step you're learning. Let's take "Find Body Pleasure" as an example since it's pretty self-explanatory; the idea is simply to feel pleasure from anything and everything having to do with your body. Concentrate on it. Bring your awareness and attention to the pleasure of walking by, reaching down, and touching the ground. In the shower, focus on the feel of the warm water on your back. Stand tall, tuck in your tummy, and inhale deeply! No matter what you do, whether it's sitting behind a desk, driving, or browsing the supermarket aisle, zoom in on the pleasure you get just from using your body.

There is nothing tiring about these exercises. In fact, you will find that learning each of these steps is an energizing process. Boosting your brain boosts your attention, your emotions, and your ability to solve problems as well.

The aim, of course, is to make the actions second nature—a way of life. Practice them as you commute to work, clean house, garden, sit at the hairdresser's, or pump gas.

Obviously, undertaking one action a day takes up about two weeks. Feel free to add actions at your own pace; you can keep adding a step a day while maintaining those you are already using, or you can double them up, then triple them up, and then use as many as possible as often as you can every day. As you do, you may note changes in your attention, awareness, energy, and emotional clarity.

Patterns of Change

A common observation among those working in the area of retraining the brain by various methods is that, paradoxically, people often are unaware that their symptom or sign of trouble disappears or dissipates. For obvious reasons, it's easier to know when a headache comes on than when it fades away.

Typically, the first change that takes place is in the most dominant or noticeable behavior that troubles you or something about you that's noticeable to others. For Ashley (she's the girl from Chapter 4 who withdrew from her chaotic family environment by snacking alone), the first noted change was increased communication: she engaged in spontaneous conversations instead of her previous standard yes-and-no answers. She had more to talk about as she began noticing more of the world around her. Amazingly, Ashley was not really aware of the changes; as far as she was concerned, she was just herself. But her new behavior, mood, and participation in the family were inescapable to other members of her family. The point is that often others around you will notice changes in your behavior before you do. Certainly, every individual is different, but chances are good that within four to six weeks, you may find that you are sleeping better. By the end of six weeks, you will start noticing changes in your eating, with substantial shifts in appetite occurring after about eight weeks. That's because your brain functions are changing your eating behavior sufficiently that your body is literally undergoing change. And that, after all, is what you're aiming for.

The OPT Program's Twelve Global Mind Fitness Tools

So let's begin.

Day 1
Mirror Healthy Living

Targets the limbic system and cingulate gyrus

The brain does what it sees. The very act of observing rewires the brain to mirror the activity or behavior being watched, looked at, seen, or visualized. Once the brain sees what healthy habits look like, it builds that into its wiring and mirrors those habits. In other words, the brain takes in what it sees and makes that happen.

The bottom line? The more healthy behavior you see, the more healthfully your brain will make you behave. When you watch people happily chowing down that turkey sandwich on whole-wheat bread, you prime your brain, constructing neural networks that will drive you to order a turkey sandwich, not a caramel sundae, the next time you are hungry. It sounds pretty simple, and it is.

Of course, the behavior in question isn't *only* about healthier eating. Positive mirroring can also help you improve your problem-solving ability, your ability to self-reflect, and your ability to assert yourself—indeed, to make any desirable changes you wish to make. That's why it's the first tool among the global brain enhancement methods and not just an eating tool.

In my view, mirroring is the most underused brain tool there is to treat self-defeating behaviors, which is why it holds the greatest potential for future treatments for weight management. It's a powerful built-in response with no learning curve.

It works in a kind and gentle way, triggering changes in eating, and effects mood automatically, bypassing the need for willful deliberation and action.

Mirror healthy living, therefore, by exposing yourself to as many healthful activities as possible. Observe healthy living scenarios. Concentrate on them. Soak up the sensory stimulation they offer you. All that you see, hear, and smell primes your brain and rewires it toward healthy activities. You can ready your brain simply by exposing it to healthy living scenarios, making it easier to carry out healthy activities.

The Science. British researchers at University College London and the Imperial College (also in London) have found that hearing someone shout triumphantly—just a simple "Yippee!" or "Yahoo!"—triggers parts of the brain's motor cortex, an area that primes us to smile. This is mirroring at work—only in this case, it is providing the glue that builds strong social bonds between people.

The brain synchronizes itself to the outside world. It alters its activity to harmonize with the rhythm of what it sees. Sometimes the rhythm is unhealthy. It's been shown, for example, that certain video games trigger the brain to put forth lingering low-frequency brainwaves and to stimulate the amygdala, which you will remember is part of the visceral brain that processes and holds the memory of emotions—including, in this case, violence and rage. In fact, there is no such thing as a scene that leaves us untouched; we have to take in enough to process scenes or reject them, but either way, for better or worse, we internalize representations of the world around us, using specialized neurons to do so.

These *specialized* neurons reproduce the activity patterns of the brain person or animal we are observing. It's a matter of "monkey see, monkey do". Ironically, mirroring was first discovered in monkeys by Iaccomo Rizzolati of the University of Parma (Italy) in 1995 when it was discovered that their brains "fired" or became active not only when they were performing a certain task, but also when they were observing someone else perform that task. When a researcher inadvertently returned to the lab eating an ice cream cone, one of the monkeys observed the action and mimicked it, activating those areas in its brain that are set in motion when licking an ice cream cone, as brain scans confirmed.

In another study, the brain activity of a runner on a treadmill was compared to that of an observer. Results showed that the observer's brain followed a similar pattern to that of the runner's; although the observer was seated, many of the areas in his brain that control muscle movement and coordination were activated.

Neural mirror systems are thought to play a major role in acquiring language skills and empathizing with others. Researchers in UCLA found that cells in the anterior cingulate are activated or "fire" when someone is poked with a needle (pain), or when watching another getting poked with a needle. In other words, mirroring is behind the ability to see and adopt another person's point of view as well as "feel their pain."

Mirroring has been hailed as one of the biggest discoveries in neuroscience in recent years. Numerous publications in the scientific and popular press attest to the excitement that mirroring has generated. The *New York Times* devoted a front page review article on the topic. While research here and abroad continues, neural mirroring is considered to be the next major discovery to help redefine theories of our nature much like the discoveries of Copernicus, Darwin and Watson and Crick (genetic code).

Mirroring could dissolve the strong sense of individualism, "us vs. them" and the barrier we perceive between ourselves and others.

Of course, mirroring is also relevant to problem behaviors such as nicotine and food addiction. When smokers are shown a picture of a bar with beer mugs, glasses, bottles, and the like, the areas of the brain associated with the anticipation of pleasure are activated. When more items associated with smoking—people smoking, ashtrays, and so on—were added in subsequent pictures, the activation in those brain areas was even more intense. The growing brain activity increased craving as well; the desire to have a cigarette grew stronger as the smoking cues increased.

The same thing happens with eating. Just looking at photos of cues we associate with eating activates the pleasure areas inside the brain and motivates us to eat. The more eating cues we see, the more powerful the brain activation and the more intense the craving.

In a recent study of more than twelve thousand people who were followed for thirty years, it was shown that people with obese friends, or family members tended to become obese. The chances of a sibling becoming obese after another sibling became obese increased by 40 percent. You might assume that genetics may be behind weight gain in the case of siblings, but the likelihood of a spouse gaining weight when the other spouse was obese was 37 percent. Further evidence that the contagious component of obesity was beyond genetics came from the finding that shows the likelihood of becoming obese increased by 57 percent if a friend became obese during a period of time. The closer the friendship—if you think of her or him as your best friend and she/he thinks of you as their best friend the likelihood of becoming obese climbs to 171 percent!

If the increase in obesity is not entirely genetic then what accounts for the "spread" of obesity? The authors' own explanation was that obesity spreads through "social ties" through the behavioral components of obesity.

In my view a huge factor behind the behavioral aspects of obesity is mirroring!

Mirroring is the mechanism that allows us to learn and be influenced from others, beyond genetics. The more time we spend together being exposed to others who mirror unhealthy behaviors the stronger the mirroring effect and the more likely to mimic their eating and lifestyle patterns. That's because with each observation of unhealthy eating your own neural networks for unhealthy eating become stronger! Once your own brain's networks are reconfigured to carry out behaviors associated with obesity—eat often, eat large portions, and highly caloric foods—then the end result is entirely predictable. You too will succumb to weight gain.

Bottom line? This study showed the powerful influence of behavioral aspects of obesity. My hypothesis for the principal mechanism by which obesity in others spreads to us, is mirroring.

With the majority of the population in the U.S. overweight, the spread of obesity not only between friends and family but also between people who simply happen to work together or live in close proximity to each other, is a force to be reckoned with.

How do you avoid becoming a victim to negative mirroring? You can't avoid being exposed to unhealthy eating behaviors, but you can take steps to resist them by optimizing your own brain through various self-regulation methods like OPT.

I see a small example of this when I work out on the stairclimber at my local health club. Usually, there is a bunch of us working out, and the climbers are lined up pretty close to one another. When I reach for my water bottle to take a drink, I count the seconds before my neighbors do the same. Amazingly, by the time I count to five, the person next to me also needs water. The same thing happens when I grab my towel to wipe my face or even when I stretch my arms up in the air.

Of course, it works the other way as well. I react in response to seeing the guy on my left taking a drink, even though I am totally aware of the phenomenon. Mimicking others is so powerful and so far out of our willful control that even a psychologist's awareness does not make me immune from its influence.

Want more proof? If you're a woman, try this experiment next time you are out with a group of women friends. Freshen your lipstick, then see how long it takes everybody else to do the same. Chances are that at least one other person will reach for her lipstick before your tube has been returned to your purse.

All of the scientific evidence is the basis of the recommendation to mirror healthy living. Mimic the people you know who eat healthfully; who stay fit at any age and in any weather; who tap into the pleasures of activities such as jumping, walking, running, getting a massage, playing sports, or meditating.

At the same time, protect yourself from unhealthy images. The flip side to positive mirroring is unwittingly mirroring the negative behaviors of others. Remember, when it comes to sensory information entering the brain, there is no such thing as zero effect. Even without your awareness, your brain takes in the information, processes it, dedicates energy to it, and is altered because of it.

That's one reason that just being out in a crowd can prove toxic. With a majority of the U.S. population today being overweight and outsized, what you see around you in public is something you do *not* want to mimic.

Yet you almost can't help it. Just looking at food or observing others while they eat triggers the activity inside your own brain to act as if it is you who is doing the eating. Images of food get your digestive juices flowing in the gastrointestinal tract after the images get the eating juices flowing inside your eating brain. Studies show that dieters are most likely to binge not when alone, but while dining at restaurants in the presence of others who are also eating. Restaurants and eating places of any kind are therefore high-risk environments, particularly if you have determined that your eating is largely driven by external cues.

I saw this reality in action at a recent seminar on weight-loss treatments. The meeting was held at eight in the evening, presumably after the dinner hour. But food was available; it is increasingly seen as an essential or a deal-sweetener in all sorts of transactions, from business meetings to academic gatherings, all of which seem to have become catered food fests. The food at this seminar was beautifully and conspicuously displayed, and all it took was for one of the event coordinators to stand up and begin eating for everyone to follow suit. One overweight person after another then proceeded to pile food onto plates, aware that they were eating but unconscious of or disconnected from the scene unfolding in front of them. The unforgettable climax of this surreal activity came at the question-and-answer session, when a beautiful obese woman raised her hand to ask the brand name of the pita chips!

Finally, keep in mind that it isn't just eating and food that provide a basis for negative mirroring. Any sort of violent, dehumanizing, obscene, or boring images can turn you from the path of healthy eating because you mirror the impulsiveness at the heart of these images. Such images strengthen the visceral brain, and an overactive visceral brain can easily overpower any input from the reflective brain (the prefrontal cortex). The result is more impulsive actions, including impulsive eating, failure to exert self-monitoring, and a loss of self-control.

Ways to Mirror. Copy the actions of the healthy eaters you know. Whom do you know who now lives the type of lifestyle you hope to achieve? Spend as much time as possible in that person's presence. Eat as many meals as you can with this person. Scrutinize as many aspects of his behavior as possible—what does he tend to eat, how often, and how much?

Don't just focus on people's eating habits. Also find out what makes them laugh, what they find exciting, what they find painful. What are their priorities? How do they handle obstacles, disappointments, illness, and hardships? How do they organize their days? Does the need to be fit come first, with the rest of the day's events planned around that requirement?

Note that healthy activities are not just workouts like walking, biking, or lifting weights, but also brain-nourishing ones like practicing yoga and meditation, visiting a museum, attending a play or an opera, reading, and learning something new. It's really about self-giving that doesn't involve food and eating.

- **Mirror magazines.** For an immediate mood boost, spend twenty minutes leafing through home, travel, fashion, or architectural design magazines. Images of rich, multicolor, tranquil landscapes, along with words that describe active, motivated, healthy, and optimistic people prime your brain to act and feel similarly. Just by reading a word, your brain has to imagine it. In order to imagine it, it has to connect with the memory of a time when you too felt active or optimistic or free, light, and strong. See? Just reading these words can prompt you to take a deep breath or relax your shoulders. So go ahead, read health and fitness, home, or sports magazines. Just looking at pictures will rouse your brain and get it started mirroring.

The more realistic the scene you observe, the stronger the brain's mimicking response and the easier you will find it to make changes toward healthier living. In terms of results, the strongest mirroring comes from viewing others in real action in real time. Three-dimensional images achieve stronger brain mirroring activation than two-dimensional images. Still, magazines and books can supply rich language and legends (word images) that can reinforce the mirroring.

• **Mirror TV and DVDs.** Use television programs and videos as other examples. Psychologists have determined that combining numerous strong stimuli into a single experience can produce a powerfully synergistic result. In fact, they refer to them as "suprastimuli." So allow your senses to be bombarded with images and descriptions of healthy people doing healthy things. Transport yourself to that scene. Try to imagine what it would feel like to be that vigorous, active person. Mirror the toned muscles and the taut abdomen. Do you feel your own posture getting straighter? Are you adjusting your tummy? Thanks to your brain, your body is likely to get in tune with the healthy specimen you're observing.

• **Visit a park or nature preserve.** You don't have to walk around; sit on a bench and just watch the people who pass by. Visit a local gym—most will give you a free day pass—and look at people of varying shapes and ages working out and socializing.

Negative mirroring. Can mirroring work the other way—negatively? You bet it can. How many times have you said to yourself, "I'm gaining weight just by looking at this dessert tray!" In a way, it's true. Since watching primes the brain to perform the observed actions, exposure to unhealthy eating or eaters can actually prompt unhealthy behavior.

So yes, looking at the dessert tray can ready your brain for eating action. In fact, any sensory stimulation involving food and eating increases the likelihood that you'll partake, whether you planned to or not. Remember that overeating takes place when you're in a state of "biological indifference"—that is, when you are not hungry but could go for something if it was within arm's reach. A desire for food, not hunger, is the drive behind biological indifference.

Here are some tips for countering negative mirroring possibilities:

• Take a pass on viewing the dessert tray or dessert menu whenever you go out to eat.

• Avoid eating with friends who eat too much or eat unhealthy foods. If you can't avoid it, make a cognitive distinction between their damaging life patterns and healthy ones, and align yourself with the healthy eater camp.

• Plan escape routes from known negative-mirroring circumstances. When others go to the office kitchen for a snack, go for a walk, catch up on your phone calls, or just close your office door and do some exercises or deep breathing to regain your calm.

• Avoid reading cooking magazines and watching cooking shows on television.

The bottom line to get the most of this most powerful technique: expose yourself to lean, athletic, healthy eaters and cheerful optimists of any age as often as possible! If not up close and personal, then in videos and magazines.

Day 2
Fortune Cookie or Mood-Induction Procedures

Works the limbic system, pleasure arc, prefrontal cortex, and frontal lobe

Words carry an implicit command. "Your heart is pure and your mind is clear"—so said my fortune cookie. At once my chest was lighter and my head less cloudy. Mood induction, or mind shifting through the use of words, is an effective way to induce desired changes in yourself or others. "Look at this brilliant, sunny day! What a boost. What a gift to wake up to. A light, shiny, bright, serene, and calm way to start this day. Sharp and clear. What a blessing!" That's all I said to my teenage son, David, as he woke up for school—not a word about his impending biology test in first period. An early-morning talk about the test—"Did you study? Are you ready?"—would not have been nearly as effective in readying him for the task ahead. Sneaky? Yes. But effective.

Since they trigger the areas in the brain that are responsible for the actual execution of the action they define, words don't just mean, they also suggest. The meaning of a word conveys a subtle message that we can't help but reenact. Words about activity and agility help energize us, while words like *slow* and *heavy* weigh us down. One research group studied people who had just solved a word puzzle with answers typically associated with being older—*frail, wise, slow, dignified*. One result of the study was that subjects walked to the nearest elevators at a slow and stately—geriatric—pace.

Words are powerful modulators of mood, attention, and behavior. With mood-induction procedures (MIPs), you can put the reality of words to work for you as a weight-management tool. Simply put, MIPs are temporarily induced emotional states; you induce a mood that will help you eat more healthfully so you can get out of the mood you are in.

The Science. Simply reading or hearing a word like *jump* triggers the areas inside the brain that are actually used in jumping. However research has shown that adding "I" statements—"I feel calm," "I feel happy," and so on—led to an even stronger tendency to simulate what is read or heard. Mood-induction procedures can be done by anyone, anytime, anywhere, and in any circumstances. They are statements you say to yourself to shift to moods in which you may be influenced to finish what you start, feel more positive, lift your energy level, grow calmer, enhance your motivation, and so forth. In short, you change to a mood suggested by the words themselves.

How do words change our mood? It turns out that when we hear or read or think of a word, the brain sets out to recognize it by searching for previous experiences involving it—images or memories that relate to that word. For example, the word *strong* evokes an image and perhaps a memory of a time when we have felt strong. In order to get all the information evoked, the brain relives that time, and neurologically speaking, it simulates or duplicates what it felt like or looked like to be strong. In other words, the areas in your brain that were stimulated when you bench-pressed a hundred pounds or lifted a heavy suitcase or carried logs inside or did anything that made you feel strong are also stimulated just by words about being strong. Remember that the brain is really a porous and empathic organ. It gathers all sorts of information that flows into it, then responds to language by evoking images, memories, and emotional connections from that flow; those images, memories, and emotions create a particular mood. "Up" moods—such as calmness or power—have been shown to be more conducive to weight management than "down" moods, so inducing up moods is an important tool in weight loss.

MIP Prescriptions. The following list of MIPs is divided into four key prescriptions to boost your overall brain strength for weight loss. Choose the memory boost prescription if you tend to get distracted, the energy prescription if you have trouble getting started, and the relaxation prescription if you are prone to anxiety. The prescription for weight loss is for everyone, so use it every day.

Prescription for Memory Boost

I am focused and aware.
I like reading.
I can remember as much as most people.
Razor-sharp memory has always been my gift.
My concentration is in top form today.
I feel like exploring the outdoors.
I can have fun working with puzzles.
I am funny and witty.
I feel that today will be very different from yesterday.
I like exploring new places and trying out
   new things.
My life is getting better and better.
I feel stronger than yesterday.
I am playful and lighthearted.

I have ample ability to thrive.
I like seeing my friends.
I can focus on counting backward by seven from one hundred.
I can remember the main news of the day.
I will be quick, alert, and attentive.
I have a sharp and focused brain.
My nature is to be strong and confident.

Prescription for Energy and Motivation

I am lively and strong.
I have ample energy.
I have abundant intellect.
I am aware and attentive.
I am a worthwhile person.
I can finish what I start.
I am powerful and alive.
I will be animated and driven.
I can transform my life right now.
I can have a fresh start.
I can become stronger.
I feel refreshed and driven to weight loss.
Exercise is healthy and fun.
I can be more active and playful.
I care about my well-being.
I embrace the fun of learning new things.

Prescription for Relaxation

I am kind and respectful to myself.
I am focused and calm.
I am slowly regaining balance.
I am friendly.

I can feel comfortable and balanced.
My face is soft, round, and smooth.
My heart is light with joy.
I know I can be carefree and playful.
Everything is fixable.
This too shall pass.
My heart is filled with gratitude.
I am serene and lucid.
My future holds many good things.
I can accomplish more by remaining tranquil.
Tomorrow will bring me a new outlook.
I will try to pause and reflect more often.
It's not possible to have the right solution for
   everything.
I will allow myself the time it takes to listen to my
   inner thoughts.
My breathing is deep and regular.
I deserve to be comfortable and peaceful.

Prescription for Weight Loss

My inner well-being depends on my diet.
My brain is my staunch ally.
Others enjoy being around me.
I will eat foods that maximize my brain's potential.
I have the privilege of being capable of improving
   myself.
I will do what I can to protect my brain from harm.
My brain can help me flourish.
I can eat less and still feel good.
My brain's resourcefulness will help me do what it
   takes to lose weight.

I can feel my brain cells thriving when I eat
   healthfully.
It's up to me to protect and nourish my brain.
When I smile, my brain smiles.
I will be more conscientious in avoiding fast food.
Taking care of my body also benefits my mind.
Together, my brain and I are a formidable alliance.
My brain makes weight loss attainable.
I will invest what it takes to obtain a healthier body.
I deserve to be leaner, stronger, healthier, and more
   lucid.
My life will be more joyful when I eat mind-boosting
   foods.
My mind is treasure.

How should you use the MIPs? I'll tell you what I do. I have typed up my selected MIPs in a large type size and have printed them out on different-colored cards. Then I've scattered them around the "landscape" of my life—that is, on the bedside table, the kitchen counter, my desks at home and at work, even on the passenger seat of my car. Each time I see one, I try to shift my mood to what the card is suggesting, knowing that the suggestion is for an emotional state that is desirable to me. I also "accidentally" drop off a card here and there in my children's rooms.

Here are some other sound suggestions about how to use MIPs, which I've gathered from patients over the years:

• Read each word, silently or aloud, with intent. Take five seconds to absorb and really think about the meaning, then pause for five seconds more before going on to the next statement.

• Make the statement or statements that describe who you strive to be into a screensaver that flashes the words randomly across your monitor.

• Just glance at your list at various intervals. That's really all it takes for your brain to pick up on the mood, although adding intent will intensify the effect.

• If you're using words instead of complete sentences as MIPs, repeat your chosen words each time you take a step—for example, as you put your left foot down, think "stronger," and as you put your right foot down, think "leaner." Use whichever words "speak" to you that day. For example, if you are going through a rough, demanding period, you might choose the words *smart* and *calm*, or *fit* and *confident*. They are more than just words; they are suggestions that your brain will try to make happen with every step you take.

In addition to specific statements and words, memories and images can also induce productive changes in mood. Next time you need a confidence booster, for example, think of a time in your life when you succeeded in overcoming an obstacle or when perseverance and determination helped you meet your goals. Is there a book or movie or piece of music that makes you feel particularly cheerful or empowered? Reach back for that feeling—either through memory or by rereading the book, watching the movie, or playing the music. Replay in your mind those times or circumstances when you felt yourself to be calmly in control and ready to undertake a transformation in your life; inducing that mood again will greatly help your weight-management efforts.

Day 3
Reboot

Works the prefrontal cortex, limbic system, basal ganglia, pleasure arc, and cingulate gyrus

When your computer stops responding, the best thing to do is shut it down and start over—reboot. The same is true of your brain where food and eating are concerned. Just close your eyes, open them again, redirect your gaze, and let your brain shift to a different frequency.

The Science. When you close your eyes, your brain automatically shifts to a neutral gear. It interprets the absence of incoming visual stimulation as a time to conserve energy and rest; it's awake but not on alert as it is when your eyes are open. The dominant brainwave pattern when your eyes are closed is the alpha wave, a frequency of eight to twelve cycles per second. Alpha wave is also the frequency the brain tends to shift to just before falling asleep and the frequency seen during yoga or meditation in people who have been practicing for many years.

Marketing experts know well how the eyes instantly seize the brain's attention, and they use that knowledge in advertising. Those pop-ups on your computer screen, for example, are annoying as can be, but they engage your brain, even if it's a brief encounter. Advertisers also know the power of such visual cues as stripes, bright colors, and fast-moving actions that capture the eye. Food advertisers know that once they have your eyes, they have your eating brain. For instance, when an image of a plate of cookies catches your eye, your attention is automatically focused on the cookies, and just about the only way to avoid the struggle that follows is simply to avoid seeing the cookies.

When that's not possible, close your eyes and reboot!

How to Reboot. In closing your eyes, you allow your brain to switch to a more relaxed, reflective mode that is much better suited to effective problem solving than to defaulting to food. At the very least, closing your eyes will allow you to become unstuck so that you can see the problem in a fresh light. Think of rebooting as the noncaloric alternative to eating. Here's how to do it:

• Close your eyes for at least five seconds, or the time it takes for four consecutive deep breaths. Breathe naturally and deeply; focus on smoothing and relaxing the area between your eyes. With your eyes closed, imagine you are looking down on your brain. Now reopen your eyes.

• Make a conscious effort to scan the horizon in all directions each time you enter and exit your home, car, or workplace. In other words, consciously reboot every time you change your environment.

• Yawn. Even when you don't feel like it, the muscles used to complete a good yawn help shift the brain's electrical activity patterns. Try yawning when you're stumped for answers during a test or when you just need to "move on" from one type of job to another, say from watching TV to balancing your checkbook.

The following exercises combine a little physical stretching with the mental stretch rebooting gives your brain:

• When you're outdoors, look over your left shoulder as far as you comfortably can, return to center, look over your right shoulder, and return to center. Now look down at your toes, then up to the sky. When you do this exercise, really look—don't just move your head.

• While you're standing or sitting, raise your arms straight up over your head, then lower them back to your sides. Do this ten times. Now close your eyes and reboot your brain.

Day 4
Use Your Imagination

Works the limbic system, prefrontal cortex, and basal ganglia

Ever since scientists learned that just imagining playing soccer or tennis gives the brain areas responsible for those sports their own form of workout, more and more practitioners have been tapping into the power of imagery to help promote healthier behaviors. Imagine yourself thin and energetic, and you can gear up your brain for the demands of weight loss, especially when the imagery is added to mirroring and MIPs.

The Science. Within the brain, there is an overlap between imagining something and actually experiencing or perceiving it. Studies using functional magnetic resonance imaging (fMRI) to identify brain locations have found a *two-thirds* overlap between the areas of the brain that imagine and those that perceive. You could say that by imagining yourself smaller and leaner, you are two-thirds of the way there. As far as your brain is concerned imagining an active, healthier, leaner, and more satisfied you, gets you two-thirds of the way to actually feeling "as if" you are experiencing those goals.

Steps to Get GITI. GITI is a process that helps activate a powerful imagery. First you generate an image. Inspect it. Transform it. Inspect it again until it is what you're seeking—in this case, a slender, fit, healthy you. In a relaxing, comfortable, quiet place, sit with your eyes closed. Take twelve consecutive breaths, filling your lungs as full as possible from your belly all the way to the top of your throat. Exhale slowly. With your eyes still closed, begin.

1. Generate an image of a fitter, leaner you engaged in a particular activity in a certain location, let's say walking upstairs in a public building.

2. Inspect that image. Does it feel genuine? Is it a possibility that you can achieve in the future? Are you totally comfortable with every detail of it? What are you wearing? What's the weather like? Let's say the sun is shining outside; you are in comfortable, loose clothes and wearing sturdy shoes. Your abdomen is tight; your posture is comfortably straight but flexible and relaxed. There is a window on every landing, and you gaze outside when you reach each floor to see how high you're climbing, as you confidently take each step.

3. Transform the image to make it more realistic. Try adding people passing you as they head downstairs; maybe they nod and smile at you.

4. Inspect the image again to refine it further. Keep on refining it, going through all the previous steps again until it is etched as clearly as possible in your mind.

Modify your techniques in your mind until you feel comfortable with the scene you have generated. Try this as often as possible throughout the day. You can use the power of imagery to conquer many self-defeating behaviors, including fear of public speaking, angry outbursts, and passivity or overcompliance.

Day 5
Find Body Pleasure

Works the limbic system, pleasure arc, basal ganglia (possibly), and prefrontal cortex (initially).

Anybody can eat and feel pleasure from the action; that's a no-brainer. The trick is to learn how to get more pleasure from all sorts of other activities. Just about every part of your body can bring you unlimited pleasure. I don't just mean the pleasure of running smoothly and effortlessly or of dancing up a storm on Saturday nights. I also mean activities like walking, touching, reaching, even breathing. By learning to tap into the sheer physical pleasures inherent in being alive, you can "demote" the pleasure of eating to just one among many, and you can demote your appetite for food to just one of many appetites. Then you'll have taught yourself to be as satisfied by touching a spring flower as by finishing off a plate of fried chicken.

The Science. "A man possesses nothing certainly save a brief loan of his own body, yet the body of man is capable of much curious pleasure," wrote novelist James Branch Cabell. We use body pleasure as a quick fix that's always at hand to combat or escape the pain of negative emotions. Sexual promiscuity, chemical abuse, and chronic overeating are some of the more common unhealthy vehicles of escaping pain through body pleasure.

Certainly, eating pleasure is cheap and available virtually around the clock; it's the old reliable standby that delivers enjoyment, optimism, and reassurance when we're feeling low. Author and scientist Mihali Csikszentmihalyi, who coined the term *flow* to describe the state of optimal experience, asserts that when the body is not "in flow," or when our inner needs

and goals are threatened or frustrated, we resort to eating pleasure: "When we are unhappy, depressed, or bored, we have an
easy remedy at hand: to use the body for all its worth." Often,
that means eating all we can.

Science therefore suggests that we cultivate other, less potentially damaging ways to bring pleasure to our lives. As it happens, human beings may well be the only animals that derive
satisfaction and pleasure from problem solving and overcoming
obstacles—their own internal obstacles or those imposed by the
external environment. We may also be the only creatures who
take pleasure from engaging our bodies. On the other hand,
looking at the self-satisfied expression of a golden retriever
who has just successfully caught the ball thrown to him, one
may want to argue that humans are not the only ones that seek
flow.

So reach beyond your basic needs. There is much joy and
pleasure to be had when you reach higher levels of physical
performance.

Practice Pleasure. Focus on the particular muscle movements
involved in each activity you do—from kicking a ball to walking
out of your apartment building to tripping the light fantastic at
your favorite club. Here are some tips to follow all day long:

- **Concentrate on relaxing during movement.** The
difference between walking in drudgery and walking in
pleasure is fluid, strong, relaxed motion. While walking or
climbing stairs, focus your attention on the sensation you
feel as the sole of each foot contacts the ground and as your
arms alternately move forward and back. Focus on your spine
as it joins and supports your head. Follow the rhythm and
chest movement of your breath. Straighten and lengthen

your spine, relax your shoulders, and allow your gaze to fall wherever it may. Note any pressure or unnatural bend in your neck, spine, or legs. Do this consistently, and you will notice that each time you move a bit closer to your goal of sensing and correcting your body movements to the point where everything flows—smoothly relaxed muscles; long, controlled strides, an abdomen that's tucked in, and a properly aligned pelvis.

• **Meditate while walking.** Many meditation practitioners prefer this method to sitting, because walking engages more diverse brain functions—those that control skeletal movement as well as relaxation breathing and awareness. There is no need for special measures; meditate as you walk to your car in a parking lot, from room to room in your home, or down the corridor at work. As often as possible, bring awareness to your bodily movements, and body pleasure will follow.

• **Set an exercise goal.** Namely, try to get a little closer to perfection with each practice. Whether it's biking, jogging, swimming, dancing, or any other activity, goals help performance. The better your performance, the more satisfying it becomes and the greater the pleasure.

• **Explore and expand your body's possibilities.** The advice I'm always giving myself is, "Throw your body at it." For example, if you haven't swum for a while, throw your body into a pool, a lake, or the sea. Don't remember the last time you climbed? Haul yourself up onto a chair or step stool, or join a hiking club and hike up a mountain this weekend. Play catch with your kid, or kick around a soccer ball.

• **Stretch.** Haven't touched your toes in a while? Reach down (bend your knees if necessary) and stay down for as long as possible. Touch the ground in front of you and gain the stability and strength that comes from this earthly connection.

• **Challenge your motor skills.** Buy a synthetic, lightweight handkerchief, toss it up in the air, and try to catch it as it floats down. Toss a ball from one hand to the other. Design your physical challenge to suit your physical ability. For example, challenge yourself to eventually scale a climbing wall or a tree as opposed to a two-step ladder.

Keep in mind that your body is the best form of physical equipment there is and the one most suited to provide you with pleasure. The more enjoyment you get from physical activities that engage your whole brain, the less you'll need to rely on that other source of pleasure—eating.

Day 6
Fit Body, Fit Brain

Works just about every area, including the pleasure arc, cingulate gyrus, basal ganglia, and the limbic system, comprising the hypothalamus and the prefrontal cortex.

The latest research on obesity rings loud and ominous warning bells: excess weight lowers the ability to learn and think. Few conditions frighten us more than losing our mental clarity and awareness, yet that is exactly what happens when we carry more weight than we should. And it happens in a variety of ways.

Certainly, the metabolism of too much high-calorie food results in high numbers of free radicals that cause tissue damage. As mentioned in Chapter 4, since the brain is the highest user of resting energy and is also highly vulnerable to toxins, it bears the brunt of this tissue damage.

Moreover, being overweight adversely affects circulation and the cardiovascular system, potentially reducing the supply of blood to the brain. But since the brain has high demands for energy—and thus for oxygen—even a slight drop in oxygen intake compromises its ability to function and thrive.

The good news, however, is that weight loss improves cognition. It's as simple as that. Certain exercises that target brain function help equip us for weight loss. That daily walk or jog doesn't just burn calories, tighten muscles, and lift our mood. It also builds the specific brain muscles in charge of memory and emotion.

The bottom line is that if you are overweight and do not exercise, you are delivering a double whammy of ill health to yourself. Your lack of exercise is no favor to your cardiovascular and immune systems, and the adverse effects to both also adversely affect cognition, so it also threatens your brain health.

It's a dire warning for Americans. Between the obesogenic foods that are dulling our senses and the lack of exercise that is causing our brains to deteriorate, we may soon find ourselves to be a nation of very big, very dumb people!

The Science. Studies show a correlation between excess weight and low IQ in children as young as two and three years of age. Since children's brains are inherently open to rewiring to ensure that they adapt in varying environments, they are easy prey to the harmful effects brought on by high-calorie foods and overnutrition. Although researchers suggest that we don't yet know all the ways excess weight harms the brain, they make it clear that being overweight or obese can make it harder for a child's brain to thrive. And since obese toddlers are five times more likely to be overweight at age twelve and throughout adulthood, the effects of obesity on cognitive impairment may be lifelong, permanently lowering the quality of life.

The following exercises demand that you use various locations in your brain. In coordinating the efforts of these areas, you are strengthening connections between your brain stem (the bottom of the brain) and your midbrain (the place where emotions are interpreted and experienced). The more these two areas "talk" to each other, the more coherent and clear your perception of yourself and the world around you is. The benefit of this widespread brain activity—apart from the obvious physical gains—is that neural networks from several brain locations are activated simultaneously, and that leads to improved awareness of your own emotions, sensations, and physical state. The word psychologists use is *proprioception*, which simply means your own perception of your body as a whole and of the relative position of various parts of your body.

Excess weight is related to reduced awareness of our own emotions—a disorder known as alexithymia—and of our own bodily state—alexisomia. Overweight people score higher for both of these disorders than do people who maintain a healthy weight. By strengthening the pathways that connect the lower-brain bodily sensations and midbrain emotions to the cerebral cortex, these exercises will enhance your awareness when something makes you feel physically or emotionally uncomfortable. That means you will be able to put your finger on what really ails you rather than using your fingers to eat something to fight the discomfort.

Balancing exercises and those that call for opposing movements are particularly important in this respect. Such movements require activation of numerous brain locations simultaneously. For balance, both the cerebellum and the brain stem are activated, as are the parietal lobes. Opposing movements—for example, moving your left arm and your right leg simultaneously—also light up multiple locations in each hemisphere of the brain: the right anterior parietal/temporal area for the left arm and the left hemisphere for the right leg. Any time you fire a bunch of brain locations in sequence or simultaneously, you establish a memory connection between those locations. With each performance of the activity, the connection becomes bigger and stronger, and your brain's flexibility and problem-solving performance improve as well.

Moreover, the hippocampus is always involved in these movements because it's where the memory of the connection is stored—the memory of both the particular muscular sequence and of the feelings associated with the movement. Although the increase in blood flow from physical activity benefits the entire brain, it is the hippocampus that we are most concerned with here. When a group of people aged sixty and older were put on a three-month regimen of daily walks, then studied by fMRI, the results showed marked increases in the size of the hippocampus and greater interconnection with other areas of the brain.

These results are not surprising. As a species, we literally evolved to think on the run—that is, we had to plan our escape from predators while running, and we had to be on the move as we thought about finding our next source of food. So the human cognitive ability is intimately tied to movement. In fact, the mere sound of the words *run, hide, jump,* or *climb* causes the brain areas associated with these activities to light up. And studies have shown that thinking about moving your body in a certain way, such as simultaneously lifting your right arm and left leg, activates the parts of the brain associated with actually performing the movement, building muscle strength as well as brain fitness. Similarly, lifting both arms up or stroking your forehead with your fingers are two simple ways to help broaden the activity inside the brain.

Body and Brain Exercises. Here are four exercises designed specifically to boost the brain for weight loss. The first three in particular are designed to strengthen the communication between the lower, middle, and upper brain areas so that all three are activated simultaneously. The level of integration among these diverse areas determines nothing less than the quality of our physical, mental, and emotional lives. We thrive on good integration; poor integration often means a life of imbalances and tribulations.

- **Walk the plank.** Stand or walk along a six- to ten-foot-long 2 × 4 beam, laid flat. Make sure you feel balanced, then walk. For a greater challenge, go barefoot, carry weights, or stretch your arms overhead. Since the "plank" is only a few inches off the ground, there should be little danger of injury if you fall.

- **Balancing act.** For this exercise, you'll need a BOSU® Ball, a balancing gadget that resembles a ball cut in half (check the website power-systems.com for information on obtaining a BOSU Ball). Set the ball down on its flat side. Now stand on the ball and try to balance. As you get better at this, try lifting one foot, then the other, or carry hand weights. Eventually, try to do squats on the ball.

- **Opposing lifts.** For this modified yoga pose, lie flat on your stomach. Slowly lift opposing arms and legs, alternating sides.

- **Walk.** Even the humble muscle movements of walking redirect the flow of energy inside the brain to areas that are underused. You know by now that, just like the body, if you leave parts of the brain unused for a long time, they atrophy.

Think of cerebral love handles that make following a healthy diet nearly impossible or a flabby limbic system that stimulates cravings and out-of-control eating because it can't deal with its routine functions.

Exercise of any kind increases the brain's capacity to generate new brain cells, strengthens existing neural connections, and protects nerve cells from injury and death. Walking is the simplest, cheapest, easiest, and one of the most effective exercises there is for accomplishing all of this.

The Last Resort. Not rushing for your gym shoes yet? Don't give up. If you can't go right to it, go around it! Consider mirroring as a first step. Feed your senses with people in motion—see them, hear them, talk to them, smell them (okay, forget the smell part). But the more you immerse your senses in a healthy-minded environment, the more extensive the mirroring. Don't be surprised to finally find yourself actually cooperating with your long-standing goal to become more active.

Does this mean you can build muscle strength and flexibility simply by imagining doing push-ups or running in your town's annual 5K marathon? Amazingly, fMRI studies show that the brain activity of people who simply observe others performing an activity the observers intend to replicate later actually begins to build the networks for these behaviors. The brains of healthy adults who lie still while watching videos of others performing various tasks become engaged as if they too were performing those tasks. Specifically, the part of the brain that allows motor learning through physical practice—the intraparietal sulcus—becomes activated. In fact, the greater the activity in the intraparietal sulcus during observation, the higher the later physical performance.

It seems that the magic of mirroring is behind the power of both imagining and intending. According to one key study, just imagining lifting your left little finger and actually lifting only the right results in increased muscle strength in the left finger. Why? Imagining this movement leads to stronger signals from the brain to the left pinkie, as measured by electroencephalogram. The pathway connecting the finger both to the muscle and to the signals from the motor areas of the brain gets stronger.

Clearly, just a few minutes of moving your body around wherever and however you choose can help strengthen the connections that can help your brain flourish. And that flourishing brain, in turn, is much better equipped to deal with the numerous wobbles that send you foraging for food. The conclusion is that for a fit brain, you need a fit body, and vice versa.

Day 7
Reroute

Works the basal ganglia, cingulate gyrus, prefrontal cortex, and limbic system

Deeply ingrained behaviors—especially those we repeat numerous times a day—are rooted in deeply engraved brain networks and pathways. We think of snacking or a sweet each time we are restless because the brain connection tying restlessness to sweets is so well developed. Such unhealthy eating is powered by rigid and predictable underlying brain patterns that leave you feeling trapped and powerless to change. It's time to break those rigid patterns so you can break free of unwanted thoughts, feelings, and actions. It's time to get unstuck.

That's what being gnarly is all about. To be gnarly is to be flexible, without being chaotic, adaptable while maintaining some sort of order. Flexibility is a key sign of a healthy, vibrant brain, a brain that's open to possibilities. Being accused of changing one's mind as if it's a character deficit is ludicrous. Changing one's mind in the face of changing reality is the epitome of intelligence. Predictability and fixed patterns of behavior are evidence of a lower level of intelligence or even evolution. Fruit flies exhibit fixed patterns of behavior; intelligent humans do not.

Unfortunately, wobbling often means loss of flexibility because it takes more energy to stay flexible than to be rigid. Wobbly or turbulent brains don't have the extra energy required for flexibility, so they tend to become trapped in predictable patterns. If you are overweight, chances are that unhealthy eating has become a predictable brain pattern. Your brain is very good at following the same unhealthy sequences over and over to the point that they're automatic—no-brainers.

The Science. Rerouting activities are physical actions whose execution and performance require the coordinated effort, or activity, of various brain locations. Rather than forcing yourself to abandon old habits of unhealthy eating, which are often deeply entrenched as well-traveled highways inside the brain (a losing proposition), you will be investing your effort in helping the brain reroute its energy to new connections. The benefit to you is that your brain will be more accepting of the lifestyle and eating changes you desire.

Rather than mandating, threatening, and pleading with the unhealthy eater inside you, you simply help your brain ease-up on its rigid patterns that have, up until now, powered your repetitive, even compulsive unhealthy eating.

Rerouting is a strategy that helps you avoid a standstill or even a confrontation between your visceral (I want bacon) and reflective (that's unacceptable and unhealthy) brain. Flexibility lets you disengage from the battle by finding options that are acceptable to both: turkey bacon?

How can you break the habitual cycle of unhealthy eating? Can you just say no and put an end to it? Everything we know about the brain's character says that simply refusing to eat poorly is not an effective way to get the results you want. You can't will unhealthy eating away, but you can go around it. Inside the brain, persistent negative thoughts, emotions, and behaviors—including eating—show up as overused pathways. You can't get food out of your mind because your brain is stuck in the deep rut of the pathway. Your brain can't shift out of the rut; instead, it keeps churning and just digs in deeper. How can you get unstuck? Reroute.

You start with some habits that are easier to change than eating. The brain learns to detour; it learns to become comfortable using an alternate route. Using your nondominant hand when brushing your teeth or emptying the dishwasher, for example, builds rerouting capabilities. It takes your brain's activity from well-traveled tracks and forces it onto new paths. The brain thus becomes accustomed to change, and that's what it needs to do in order to transform its deeply ingrained, unhealthy connections to food.

Rerouting Exercises. Here are some tips for starting the rerouting of your brain:

- **Left is right.** If you are right-handed, hold your toothbrush in your left hand, or vice versa if you are left-handed. Ditto for reaching inside a cabinet, taking clothes out of the dryer, and brushing your hair. You get the point.

- **Try yoga or tai chi.** Both practices are very important in helping forge and strengthen balance connections.

- **Alter your routine.** If you always start your day with the same rituals in the same sequence—get up, brush your teeth, shower, have breakfast, read the newspaper in a particular order—try reversing them or mixing them up. Change your clothing style. Listen to music you don't normally listen to.

- **Reflect on unaccustomed ideas.** Consider creationism, the legalization of marijuana, or required military service for all. Play devil's advocate, and try to see the other side of your usual argument.

- **Use your eyes.** Make a conscious effort to scan every direction when you are walking or just resting. Direct your eyes up, down, left, and right.

- **Shift your furniture.** Move it around the same room for a new look, or rotate items from room to room. Take gradual steps away from your "typical" style. Go out without makeup; change your hairstyle or the color palette of your clothing.

- **Adjust your brain language.** The unique way you use language, the words you use to describe your experiences in the world has a powerful influence on your emotions and behavior. Your language compels the brain to duplicate the implicit meaning of the words you use: "I will never lose this weight" primes the brain to pursue it as a goal to make it happen; to assure that you indeed don't ever lose this weight. It's best to think of your verbal expressions as suggestions! Avoid extreme words and expressions such as *always, never, no way, constantly, all the time, most definitely,* or *certainly.* "I find chocolate irresistible" leads the brain to try and make it so you can't resist. Try to use flexible language: "I think so." "I need more time to consider or reflect." "Sometimes." "Can you tell me more about it?" "Why do you think that?" "I'm flexible. Let's see if there is another way."

Day 8
Apply Cognitive Control (the Brain Brake)

Works the prefrontal cortex, limbic system, and pleasure arc

Have you ever marveled at other people's self-control while quietly condemning your weak-willed genes as you bite into that second piece of cake? What's their secret? Most often, it's the brake pedal in the prefrontal area of the brain. That's the area that's primarily responsible for cognitive control, for pausing long enough to inhibit unwanted impulses, including eating. Your brain brake probably hasn't been used for a while and may have lost some of its vigor and strength, but rest assured, it is there.

Unlike the brakes in your car, which wear out with use, the brain's braking system gets stronger the more you use it. If giving in to unwanted eating is more the rule than the exception for you, chances are your brain brake has grown weak and sluggish; it can no longer forego or delay gratification.

The Science. The neural network that controls eating and cravings is pliable; that is, it can be influenced by a variety of factors. Maternal nutrition can be ground zero for weight gain. Recent findings show that the brain's eating mechanisms are determined in part by a mother's nutritional state before giving birth. These findings demonstrate that the pattern of overeating, including the inability to forego unwanted eating, may be due to maternal energy overload. This can rewire the eating brain, intensifying cravings for certain foods, making self-restraint difficult, and actually weakening the brain's braking system.

Another line of research shows that overweight dieters are more prone to engage in behaviors such as alcohol abuse or addiction, smoking, shoplifting, and sexual recklessness than are nondieters of average weight. Obviously, all of these harmful behaviors are associated with poor impulse control. Take another look at your answers from the wobble test concerning the prefrontal cortex, which controls your ability to pause and consider any behavior before undertaking it. If you have several positive answers, your overeating is probably only part of a pattern of risky behaviors brought on by poor impulse control.

No discussion about cognitive control can be complete without bringing in studies that show what goes on inside the brains of people who have a hard time saying no to a second piece of chocolate cake. Research indicates that people who find cognitive restraint difficult exhibit higher than normal activity in an area of the brain known as the left ventral striatum. These people tend to find food more stimulating than others do and therefore difficult to resist. In other words, it's the particular wiring of the eating brain that makes it difficult for these people to refuse a second helping of cake again and again. As we mentioned in Chapter 2, the best brakes can fall short at the onslaught of intense desire. That's why working on all parts of the brain to achieve balance is so important. A balanced brain doesn't fluctuate too intensely.

But even if your eating brain is wired to overeat, your mother was overweight, or you have little impulse control, it doesn't mean that your eating can't be curtailed. It means that you need to become more selective about which foods you allow into your body. Recognize that your eating brain has unwittingly been hijacked by your stomach: too much food and too much high-calorie food. You can help reclaim your eating brain and help rewire it to the way nature intended by strengthening your brain brake and applying the other brain-retraining tools. Your brain will learn from experience and use what it has learned to put a stop to bad eating habits effortlessly; you won't even have to think about it.

Brain Brake Techniques. Delaying or inhibiting eating is the most difficult thing to accomplish; it's literally at the top of the difficulty hierarchy. To boost your brain brake, therefore, don't try starting at the top. Instead, begin by pausing or inhibiting less pleasurable actions. Every time you pause before taking any action that will bring you pleasure, you strengthen your brain brake. Stretch out the delay or stop yourself altogether from buying that gorgeous new pair of shoes, and your brain brake will soon be strong enough to delay or forego the gratification of even the first piece of cake.

When you're ready to move on to eating, start by trying to delay your food gratification rather than forego it completely. That's basic training for strengthening your brain brake. Let's say it's breakfast time, and you're hungry. Oatmeal is on the menu, and you naturally reach for the instant oatmeal because it's faster; you can't wait for the old-fashioned, slow-cooking, steel-cut kind. After all, eating is not the issue; you will be eating oatmeal either way. Time is the issue.

But try thinking of the time problem another way. Since the brain is sure that it will be eating shortly, it can be more patient. Moreover, switching to slow-cooking oatmeal has other benefits. The steel-cut grind is harder for your body to break down. The slower release of glucose into your bloodstream lowers the glycemic index, resulting in more stable blood sugar fluctuations and helping to curb cravings and overeating. In other words, you'll eat less if you wait for the slow-cooking, steel-cut variety.

But suppose you're not facing breakfast or oatmeal. Suppose it's four in the afternoon and a plate of cookies is being passed around at the office. Can you wait a minute before you take the cookie? If so, you can probably wait two minutes. Know that you can have a cookie if you want it but continue waiting anyway. Think about how the world won't end if you don't eat that cookie. Shift your brain's activity from "I want a cookie" to "How many calories, fat, and sugar are in those cookies?" Simply thinking about facts will help your brain shift its focus away from the cookies. So will doing a multiplication table (nine times two is eighteen, nine times three is twenty-seven, and so on), or looking at the clock and waiting five minutes. Close your eyes. After a while, you may find that you don't want a cookie after all. This is what can happen when you put a little time between you and whatever you're about to put in your mouth.

To start strengthening your brain brake, devise an agenda and plan for delaying, foregoing, and/or inhibiting the things and activities you desire and tend never to put off. Here are some of the tricks I use:

• **Postpone.** Since I tend to watch television instead of studying, walking, cleaning, helping around the house, or paying bills, I limit my TV time to thirty minutes at a time.

• **Delay.** I wait a day (or more) before I buy a dress I have my eye on. During the day of waiting, I ask myself these questions: Do I need the dress? Can I afford it? Can I do without it?

• **Cook slower.** I don't use the microwave just so I have to wait longer to eat. I cook in the oven or on the stove.

- **Seconds delay.** I pause twenty minutes before eating a second portion. By then, maybe I won't want to eat it at all.

The brain brake's good intentions often need support. Here are some tips on how to distract yourself from unwanted eating:

- **Reroute.** Chew a piece of gum.

- **Escape.** Leave the foodscape—avoid restaurants, fast-food drive-ins, food halls, and the like.

- **Eliminate temptation.** Throw away any food you just can't help but eat.

- **Work before play.** Try to limit or postpone your "wants" in noneating situations: try cleaning out your garage, sort through a closet, or follow up on a bill before doing something you enjoy.

- **Inquire.** Ask how and why. No matter what the question, your brain will use the frontal and prefrontal cortex to come up with the answer, adding strength to the brain brake.

Day 9
Create a Pleasant Environment

Works the limbic system, prefrontal cortex, and pleasure arc

Although the brain is in charge when it comes to what you eat, it has no stomach of its own. So how does it find nourishment? As we have seen, the brain thrives on a menu of diverse experiences. A baby's brain doesn't grow from food alone; it also needs the nourishment of an enriching and stimulating environment. You may occupy a bigger body than a baby, and it may take different types of stimulation to amuse you, but your brain still needs a healthy balance of challenge and positive sensory stimulation.

The Science. Neurobiological research has established the interplay between the brain and social and environmental experiences. Stress and a drab environment are bad news for neurons and make the brain sluggish. And a sluggish brain is a powerful root cause of excessive eating. If you feel angry, pressured, sad, unloved, alone, afraid, or uncomfortable, you are paying a heavy toll twice: first, because those negative emotions are painful, and second, because your brain is curling up and shrinking—and probably defaulting to eating to find comfort.

How can you use your environment to boost your mental performance? A classic study performed in Israel provides an answer. The study's authors distributed automatic teller machines (ATMs) randomly in various locations around the country. The machines were identical in design, but some were brightly colored and had textured surfaces, while others were gray and dull with smooth keys. The study then compared the number of transaction errors in the colorful, textured machines to those in the plain ATMs. Predictably, the attractive machines had fewer errors.

Why "predictably"? We've long suspected that happy, positive people perform better, and we know that attractive things help boost mood. The connection between attractive things in the environment and improved performance is serotonin and dopamine—the feel-good neurochemical duo. Beautiful objects and feelings of joy and optimism boost the levels of both of these neurotransmitters, which in turn enhances performance.

Music that you like can contribute to a positive brain environment. It "soothes the savage breast" precisely because it soothes the brain. Music shifts brain activity to different locations and alters electrical frequency. The ancient Greeks thought certain rhythms and melodies could cure gout and insanity. It's not as far-fetched as it sounds, considering that music can increase or decrease autonomic activities such as respiration, blood pressure, and muscle tension. It improves memory by balancing the autonomic nervous system, activating groups of neurons to work together more harmoniously. Music has been shown to benefit overall health and the immune system, enhance language skills, and of course, stir emotions. Any music that you enjoy listening to is healthy for your brain.

Good smells also provide a pleasant environment for your brain. Scents existed before consciousness. Long before humans could use language to communicate, they relied on scent as a means of motivation and emotion. The olfactory system is yet another limbic function with connections to the hippocampus and amygdala. You don't necessarily have to be aware of a smell to be affected by it. Lavender relaxes your brain, affecting the limbic system, and alters your brain's electrical activity and physiology even if you don't notice it, let alone see it.

How powerful is scent? Dr. Alan Hirsch concocted a scent that increased the time a person spent gambling in Las Vegas by anywhere from 33 to 53 percent; those who were exposed to the scent spent more money. Department stores use odors that can prompt you to spend more time shopping. Some smells affect memory; at important events in China, it's the custom to pass around bowls filled with a unique scent to ensure that people remember the event.

Making Your World Brain-Beautiful. Positive sensory stimulation, such as vibrant colors, complex geometric designs, or soft, round objects, engage the brain in ways that lead it to grow more cells and strengthen those already in use. Remember that our ability to perceive color is a relatively new skill for our species; it ties into the bran's thirst for complexity and appreciation of creative quests, like the ability to imagine.

Enriching your environment by varying colors, shapes, and textures is one of those brain-boosting actions that can easily be dismissed for not being "scientific" enough. But overlooking the feeding of your brain with sensory input is akin to feeding it junk food or too little food; it can survive, but it cannot possibly thrive and grow.

Many of the regulation tools you've already learned will help you feed your brain. Spending at least thirty minutes of every brain-training day doing movement exercises—anything from dancing to stretching to tai chi to weight lifting to cycling—nourishes the brain and helps it flourish. But feed your senses with pleasurable stimulation as well. The more you touch, smell, see, and hear in your daily environment, the more the brain thrives. Make an effort to expose your senses to as many different experiences as possible, as often as possible, but stop before you feel overwhelmed.

As much as you can, gently turn your attention to experiences that you find pleasurable. Make a list of activities you enjoy and begin incorporating at least one into each day. A happy brain performs better and is quicker to arrive at creative solutions to problems.

I think of experiencing pleasure and joy in everyday sights, smells, and sounds in terms of minimum daily requirements for brain fitness. Here are some ways you can ensure that you take your vitamins:

Nurturing Activities

• **Smile.** Even if you are grouchy, forcing yourself to smile helps improve your mood. That's because the muscles you activate when you smile cause areas in your brain to turn on and release serotonin and dopamine, the feel-good neurochemicals.

• **Surround yourself with beauty.** Sometimes one look at your favorite scarf, that beat-up old teakettle you love, or the coffee table on which your baby first pulled himself upright can make you feel better; it's all you need to spark your brain to a pleasant memory and give the hippocampus a new burst of energy. Certain objects and landscapes have an inherent ability to make us subjectively happy. Think of the shape of a "smart car" or Volkswagen bug. The smoothness of their contours, their roundness, along with the colors and "bug eyes," may or may not prompt you to want to own one, but they are likely to bring a smile to your face; you are just glad that such things exist. They combine many of the features we are prewired to find enjoyable. Your brain naturally secretes the feel-good chemicals that help it regenerate new cells and new connections. If smooth, round objects are pleasing to your touch—and studies show they're pleasing to most of us—pick up a well-worn pebble.

• **Let your brain follow your nose.** Immerse yourself in the smells you enjoy, but remember that sweet smells like lavender and vanilla have a powerful trophic or nurturing influence on the brain. That's because they trigger neurochemicals and hormones that have healing and restorative properties. Here is another trick: tie a memory to a smell and you are bound to hold on to that memory forever! To keep things organized, not to mention sweet smelling, you need to use one scent per memory.

• **Heart-smart is brain-smart.** A diet high in antioxidants, complex carbohydrates, and whole grains as well as low in meat is as good for your head as it is for your heart—especially when you emphasize foods high in omega-3 fatty acids. The BrainMed program in Chapter 7 is just such a diet plan. Once again, remember to be as careful with what goes into your mouth as you would be about feeding a young child. Your body will keep running on unsuitable fuels like artificial sugars, trans fats, and animal fats, but it will not flourish. These foods make your body unhealthy and overweight, and they make your brain sluggish and dull. Avoid them.

• **Mozart for adults.** Who hasn't been affected by a music box or the classical pieces played during the Fourth of July fireworks? Music entrains, or transports, the brain; its tempo, rhythm, and other sound qualities trigger shifts between different areas that allow us to feel various emotions. A little known fact is that the brain has "harmonics" of its own; many scientists think it uses a scale seven! In other words, the brain evolved to read information by changes in its own rhythm or frequency. Turn on your iPod, radio, or CD player and do your own brain entrainment to get the brain activity you desire. Most bookstores carry CDs designed to help your brain with sleep, motivation, energy, and even learning.

Activities to Stimulate and Challenge Your Brain

• **Read.** Almost everything about reading is good, but strive for a balance between nonfiction and fiction. Remember that humor and satire, or wit, are brain boosters.

• **Learn.** Memorize a list of new words, or look up unfamiliar words in a crossword puzzle. Learn a new route to a restaurant or other place you visit often. Be aware of both global and local events. Play the "country mouse and city mouse" game—if you live in the city, explore the suburbs or a rural area; reverse the process if you live in the suburbs or country.

• **Work puzzles.** Do the "math," such as Sudoku, or word puzzles. Both stimulate and challenge your brain, helping it to thrive.

In my view, beauty, intellect, and kindness expressed in our emotions and actions and a beautiful, enriching environment are what give life its color and meaning. They are powerful tools that you can use to bring pleasure and peace into your world as well as to diffuse a negative atmosphere in your home or office. Finally, the age-old question "Does a clean car drive better?" has an answer: yes, it most certainly does! A vehicle that's freshly washed and better smelling triggers happy brain chemicals and hormones that in turn sharpen your driving skills and widen your appreciation of passing landscapes. Who wants to ruin chemistry like this by shouting and beeping the horn at the person who cut you off?

The other, even more important question is "Why does cheap wine taste better in crystal goblets?" The beauty of the glass enriches the color of the wine. These sensory pleasures trigger the neurochemical soup in your brain that boosts the taste. Who needs Dom Perignon? Spend your money on Baccarat instead.

Day 10
Think Left for Joy, Right for Worry

Works the frontal lobe and prefrontal cortex

When we feel joyful and optimistic, it's because the left prefrontal cortex of the brain—the area above the left eyebrow—is activated. High activity levels in the right prefrontal cortex, however, correlate to feelings of pessimism and negativity. Therefore, to boost joy and optimism, it's helpful to boost the activity in the left prefrontal cortex.

The Science. Can you think of an event in your life that left you feeling particularly happy, confident, and satisfied? If only you could relive such moments and feel as you did then—when you first fell in love, for example, or first saw your newborn's face. But the first time cannot be duplicated, and the second time is always slightly less pleasurable than the first.

Still, science tells us that every pleasurable event leaves a trace inside the brain, and researchers now believe that our brains may someday evolve to the point of allowing us to relive an entire event—pleasure and all—through that trace, simply by evoking the memory.

That's in the future. For now, neuroscientists have at least identified the brain locations of key emotional and physical functions, and fMRI scans confirm that left is for joy, and right is for worry. When the left prefrontal cortex is underactive—when its frequency goes down to alpha waves (eight to twelve cycles per second)—that leaves the right side unbalanced. The resulting dominance in the right prefrontal cortex correlates with negative emotion. The infants of mothers with depression tend to have less left prefrontal cortex activity than infants whose mothers are not depressed. When the alpha frequency increases in the left prefrontal cortex, however, symptoms of depression have been shown to dissipate. Therefore, the aim is to alter the brain's electrical patterns, sending the flow of energy to specific locations. We can do this with a number of different techniques, including meditation—and the meditation-like tools in this section—yoga, hypnosis, and neurotherapy.

By altering brainwave patterns, we alter our emotional and cognitive states. And since eating is influenced by our emotional and cognitive states, the tools here can bring us to healthy eating in two ways—first, by helping reduce the emotions that tend to throw us into the unhealthy feeding mode, and second, by engendering the emotional state that correlates with healthy eating.

Left with Joy Techniques. Use the following steps to help stimulate feelings of happiness:

1. Slowly close your eyes. With them closed, try to look down, as if you are trying to look into your brain.

2. Focus on your breathing, keeping it calm and regular. Each breath carries oxygen and nutrient-rich blood into your brain, bathing it with life-boosting elements that help it grow healthy.

3. With your eyes still closed, look up at the left corner of your brain—the area above your eyebrow—and behind it. Can you touch that area with your fingers? Can you direct your attention and energy to that area?

4. Imagine this area to be a beautiful, calm, but very busy place.

5. Nourish it by saying and thinking about the meaning of words like *ample, optimal, powerful, serene, active,* and *intricate* to boost the energy flow to this area.

6. Imagine a symphony going on in your brain. Each instrument is energy that shows up as a dot of light. Visualize dots of light dancing all over this area.

7. Try to focus on that spot and concentrate on making it like an orchestra: orderly, organized, and harmonious.

8. Stay focused on the left prefrontal cortex as long as is comfortable. Try to remember what it feels like to make this area a busy, comfortable, orderly place, and revisit as often as you can.

9. Release your focused, calm attention whenever you're ready. Open your eyes and take four consecutive deep (belly) breaths, exhaling slowly.

In addition to this focusing exercise, you can help boost your neural networking capabilities by encouraging a wide range of activity inside your brain. Networking is essential for a balanced brain because the networks integrate all the varied information the brain receives.

Here's an exercise I do while walking or pedaling on a stationary bike. With my eyes open or closed, I visualize my brain as a power generator, sending out free-flowing energy that empowers everything it touches. Next, I direct this energy to the area above my left eyebrow and imagine the tissue there enriched with vital nutrients and brain-boosting neurochemicals. I think of empowering words to help the process along—*life force, strength, confi-*

dence. The words help me send even more of these qualities to my upper left brain. I feel lighter and more confident, and my breathing, though fast from the walking or biking, is regular and comfortable. Suddenly, my mind drifts to the potentially problem-filled work meeting that looms later in the day, and I sense my anxiety rising. I gently remind myself that the chemicals from my unpleasant feelings are hurting my brain and gently suggest letting go of these feelings. I ask myself firmly, "Is this problem worth killing your brain over?" I visualize the brain above my right eyebrow and try to slow it down and make it quiet, so the left side can prevail. Unhindered once again, the energy continues to move from place to place in my brain, leaving me feeling comfortable, calm, and in the moment.

Day 11
Single-Task

Works most major brain areas

In a world where multitasking can be anything from an unavoidable necessity to a status symbol advertising self-importance, single-tasking may be seen as mundane at best, obsolete at worst. But we cannot progress faster or further than the brain can go. Given our neurological setup, single-tasking is the most efficient and comfortable way to tackle tasks.

It's simple. We just don't have the brain architecture to carry out several tasks at once without compromising the quality of our performance. But we do have the brain architecture that lets us think we can, which probably accounts for why so many of us keep on doing it.

Multitaskers live life bouncing from stimulus to stimulus without staying long enough to connect to anything. Unfortunately, all this bouncing around makes it hard to know what you ate, how much you ate, or how it tasted. For that matter, it makes it hard to connect to your true body size and shape. Moreover, you miss out on the inherent pleasure that results when you strive to be the best at what you are capable of doing, feeling, and thinking. And you know what happens when emotional pleasure drops: you tend to eat for pleasure.

Doing one thing at a time is more natural and more consistent with the brain's makeup than multitasking. It also results in a more coherent experience of what's going on in the present—the time between the "not yet" and the "no more." Single-tasking allows for a tighter connection between the external and internal environment, and this boosts the richness and depth of your experiences.

The Science. Scientists have long known that the brain cannot do two things at once. If it tries, the queue of incoming information jams up and forms a bottleneck as it waits to be processed. The areas of the brain where this bottleneck occurs have been identified as the lateral, frontal, and prefrontal cortex.

The fact is that we cannot process two things simultaneously; there is always a time lag, so the idea of multitasking is a bit of a misnomer. What really happens is that the brain shifts attention from one task to the next. In other words, rather than doing three things at once, your brain divides its energy; it is in transit, moving from task to task. Since it gives attention only briefly to any single thing you are doing, you are clearly not performing as well as you might on any task.

In a way, multitasking is a disservice to yourself, because your performance is not as good as if you were to focus on one thing at a time. As to the argument that multitasking saves time, it turns out that it probably costs you more time because you end up having to do things over—too many mistakes, too many gaps.

Moreover, subpar performance typically results in time crunches and a disorganized lifestyle that leave little time for such luxuries of self-maintenance as eating healthfully and exercising regularly. Cooking from scratch and proactively planning healthy meals are out the window!

All of this also tends to mean lower self-esteem, which is fertile ground for emotional eating. Since multitasking often leaves us absentminded or not as consciously aware as we should be, we also have less protection against foodscape cues. We just proceed on automatic, and the visceral brain takes over. Disengaged from the prefrontal cortex that allows for top-down actions, we can mindlessly reach for yet another candy bar or peanut butter sandwich, without regard for the consequences. This is one reason that single-tasking is being taught to bulimic and binge-eating women at Griffith University in Queensland, Australia, and has been shown to improve symptoms of anxiety, depression, and stress-related physical and emotional problems.

Ways to Single-Task. Building single-tasking skills can be done in a variety of ways:

• Place a raisin in your mouth and keep it there for as long as possible. Try to be conscious of its presence, but resist the temptation to bite and swallow. You may substitute a piece of gum or a jelly bean.

• Slow down the pace of your everyday activities—eating, walking, unloading the dishwasher, and brushing your teeth.

• Focus your attention on one task at a time, whatever it is, by silently repeating, "This is all I can be doing right now," or "I can only do one thing at a time well."

• Designate specific times to work on projects, even if they are recreational—time to work in the garden, time to call a friend. When the time comes for that activity, focus completely on it, and let go of what's next on your agenda. Right now, you are just where you need to be.

• Use single-tasking to help you slow down when you feel anxious, tired, or emotionally raw or when you just need to find the pleasure inherent in whatever you are doing.

• Avoid multitasking, especially when the tasks you are trying to do require heavy sensory involvement, such as carrying on a phone conversation while reading your e-mail or surfing the Net. While you're on the phone, move to a room that doesn't have access to the Internet or a TV.

• Whenever possible, designate a specific place for a single major activity: the car for driving (a novel idea), the bedroom for sleeping, the desk for working. Then remove any item that competes for your attention (out of sight, out of mind). At your place of work, keep snacks in the common eating area, not on your desk or in a drawer. Needless to say, *dashboard* and *dining* shall not be joined together.

• Avoid mental multitasking. You may not be doing three things at once, but you're thinking about doing the next three things on your list. Recognize that this is just as detrimental to your well-being as actually carrying out three projects simultaneously. Gently remind yourself of your right to think of only one job at a time.

In my experience, once you give yourself permission to do just one thing at a time and do it well, you are not likely to go back to multitasking. That's because single-tasking feels so good. The brain doesn't like the back-and-forth and pressure of being rushed inherent in multitasking, and neither do you. Once you experience the pleasure that comes from doing one thing at a time, you may find that you go on the alert and become very defensive when anyone tries to throw more things at you.

Day 12
Mindfulness

Works the frontal lobe, prefrontal cortex, limbic system, and basal ganglia

Meditation and mindfulness go hand in hand. That's because the emotional, physical, and cognitive state of being mindful is a basic building block in meditation. Researchers at Emory University are finding that a type of ancient spiritual practice, Zen meditation, gradually changes brain structure and can be of potential benefit in the treatment of Alzheimer's and attention deficit disorder (ADD).

The Science. Functional magnetic resonance imaging has shown that meditation practiced over a long period of time increases activity in areas of the cerebral cortex that pertain to attention and memory. For the first time, researchers at the University of Wisconsin–Madison found that "mindfulness meditation" led to improvements in the immune system as well as brain function. Mindfulness treatments were deemed to be powerful therapy for stress and anxiety, key causes of decreased immunity. As part of this study, the electrical activity of the brain was also recorded in the frontal areas of the brain, and meditation increased the activity in the left frontal area. (Another reason to keep on thinking "left for joy.")

Meditation helps build brain muscle, adding to the thickness of the outer layer of the brain, which suggests that people who meditate may see improvements in their thinking, sensory processing, and emotional stability. Mindfulness and meditation are "practices," and as such, they need to be individualized to suit your temperament and lifestyle. Mindfulness is a way of living each minute; you can bring it into everything you do, from breathing to taking out the trash. While meditation may affect your daily actions, including your posture and breathing, it's usually done at specific times of the day.

There is an abundance of resources to help you get started with meditation, but I especially like *The Meditative Path*, by John Cianciossi, as a general beginner's guide and *Zen and the Psychology of Transformation*, by Hubert Benoit, as a guide to Zen meditation. Finally, *Learn to Relax*, by Mike George, offers a practical guide to relaxation as well as visual stimulation to help you feel serene.

Mindfulness Activities. There are many options to open up your brain's mindfulness area, which you'll find here:

• Make a decision to be more aware but less judgmental of everything you do, every move you make.

• Slow down all your actions. Initially, the unfamiliarity may make you uneasy, but you'll quickly adjust to the new rhythm.

• Neutralize intrusive thoughts that get in the way of your awareness by using a single-tasking mantra: "This is my time for mindfulness. I will think about that later."

• Begin mindfulness training with your breathing. Sit comfortably and focus on the length of your inhalations and exhalations; is one longer than the other? Notice anything that stands out while you breathe. Do you have intrusive thoughts? Strain while inhaling? Brief exhalations and rapid, shallow breaths? In the beginning, you play the role of a caring observer, taking in information. In time, you become a healer and make gentle suggestions for changes to your breathing. You may suggest deeper inhalations and longer exhalations. If you feel depleted and low in energy, allow or coax your exhalations to be brief. If you are on edge and need to slow down, focus on prolonging your exhalations.

• Bring mindfulness to walking. This action works well with the suggestions for body pleasure (Day 5). Focus on your body and anything else in your environment that draws your attention.

• When turning partially or completely around, notice if some of your body turns before the rest follows. Are your torso and hands still in their original positions while your eyes and the rest of you have "gone on" to a different scene? Make adjustments to be sure that your whole body turns together— from one task to the next.

• Take time to absorb your surroundings and how you fit within those surroundings while going about your daily routine—waiting for your meal at a restaurant, dancing at a party, sitting behind your desk, or standing in front of your stove or sink.

• To maintain mindfulness, lower your shoulders and take four consecutive deep breaths—two with your eyes open, and two with them closed.

By now you can see that meditation is boosted by mindfulness and mindfulness by single-tasking. All the OPT actions blend to produce a gestalt; the result is greater than the sum of its parts. By using all the OPT tools, you keep adding benefits that help improve brain function, leaving fewer reasons for the brain to trigger overeating. You will get faster results by working on all the brain areas at once.

Your Ample, Thriving Brain

You've completed the first part of your training program. Hopefully, you have found these actions much more enjoyable and easier to carry out than sticking to any diet. Implementing these steps will help you follow a healthy eating regimen with less effort on your part. You do your part of applying the OPT tools, and your brain will reward you by making healthy eating easier. In just a few weeks, you may also notice improvements in other areas of your life, such as better sleep, memory, and mood. Be sure to incorporate the actions that help you the most into your daily routine for the best possible results. Now, on to the eating tools.

6

Retraining Revisited

Eating Neuroregulation Tools

With the regulation tools as a strong base, you're now ready to learn the eating tools of the OPT program. As with the twelve tools for overall brain health, the ten eating regulation tools are designed to help you build the most important trait there is for weight loss and healthy weight maintenance: self-regulation. It is this trait that will enable you to stop overeating and, facing a choice, to opt for carrots rather than cake as a snack.

All of these tools enhance your ability to plan, problem solve, and focus your actions on a goal. In this case, the basic global tools plus the eating-focused ones you are about to learn will help you focus your actions to meet your weight-loss goal.

But there is even more to it than that. Self-regulation, the ability to control impulses, enhances your ability to manage every aspect of your life. In fact, it has been shown to be a more important predictor than IQ for success in life—even for academic success. Of course, the success you are most interested in today is the success of retraining your eating brain so you can lose the weight you want.

Clear the Decks

You're about to effect major changes in your life. Before you start this part of your program, it's time for some prep work. Because it's always good to begin something new with a clean slate, now is a good time to get rid of some of the clutter in both your life and your eating.

Clean Your House

Start by cleaning house—literally. Head for the kitchen and get rid of the fatty meats in your freezer. Leave fresh or frozen fish; chicken breasts; lean cuts of beef and pork such as tenderloin; and ground chicken, beef, or turkey that's less than 7 percent fat. Leave canned tuna or sardines. Unless you have a schedule that does not allow you to invest fifteen to twenty minutes for meal preparation, there is no need for frozen or prepared meals. They may not be high in calories, but they often lack nutritional value. You can do better with about the same amount of effort it takes to microwave them.

Now, on to the harder job: cleaning your pantry. In the American household, the pantry is the most likely storage place for simple carbohydrates. That's a good thing, because you won't have as many search-and-destroy missions. The easiest way to know what to throw or give away is to aim for manufactured foods that contain the three most common sources of simple carbohydrates and saturated fats:

- White flour
- White rice
- White sugar

Here are some examples of what must be removed:

- Cookies; cakes; white bread; bagels; muffins; pancake or waffle mixes; pasta, orzo, and noodles other than those made with whole wheat

- Candy, potato chips, any crackers that aren't stone-ground whole wheat, fried flour tortilla chips

- Any sodas that aren't sugar-free, any juice that isn't labeled as 100 percent pure juice from your refrigerator

Make sure you remove:

- Fatty meats such as bacon and sausage, ground meat with more than 7 percent fat

- Whole-fat dairy products, cheeses made with whole milk (cheddar, brie, parmesan)

You will have a much easier time managing your eating when you don't even have to look at unhealthy foods, so either donate them to the local food pantry or throw them away. If you feel guilty, ask yourself the question I put to myself one day as I stared at a platter of beautiful Christmas cookies I had just unceremoniously tossed into the wastebasket: "Would you rather they were inside you?"

Clean Your Body

Once you've cleansed your home of the kinds of foods you know you don't want to eat, do the same with your body: give it a time-out from high-calorie and manufactured foods and from overeating. Think of it as a washing-out process—the same sort of thing commonly done for people who have taken multiple medications over a long period of time. The idea is to give the body a chance to detoxify and learn to function without the constraints of drugs; in your case, the washout helps you ease off the effects of lots of calories.

Another reason for the cleansing is to regain your sense of taste. Long-term consumption of junk foods dulls your taste and appreciation for natural foods to the point that it becomes difficult to enjoy their subtle flavors. A washout gives your taste buds time to recover from this taste desensitization.

How should you cleanse your system?

• Strive to have one day of just water, hot tea, and fruit. If you can't tolerate it, add almonds or more fruit.

• Keep away from sweets and flour for as long as you can manage, but at least for a full day.

• By far the most effective technique—and it's easier to do than most people expect, certainly easier than limiting portions—is to fast. A period that's completely free of food definitely cleans out your system, reinvigorates your taste buds, and calms your appetite markedly. It's the most comprehensive, albeit drastic, way to clear the decks for retraining your eating brain.

Fresh Thinking About Eating

As you prepare to make the eating changes your retrained brain will demand, it's a good idea to start focusing on some core facts of healthful eating.

Ban Certain Foods

It's easier to make up your mind that certain food categories like sweets or fast foods are just not an option for you than to ponder "Should I or shouldn't I?" every time you're faced with these foods. For example, I no longer have an internal debate on which fast-food item to order for my teenaged son because I made the decision long ago that the whole category of fast food is blocked; it is simply not to be considered as an option. It's easier that way.

Think about it. If you're a guest in someone's home and you find loose change in the guest bedroom, are you tempted to take the money? Do you go back and forth, agonizing over whether you should or shouldn't take it? Of course not. The thought of stealing is automatically and unconsciously rejected at the midbrain level, so you're not even aware of it. The decision-making process—that we don't take things that don't belong to us, and it's not an option—takes place before it rises to the level of awareness.

You can do the same thing with certain categories of food that you know are unhealthy. Label them as "not an option," and tell yourself, "I don't go there." You'll see. In a short time, your brain won't even consider them.

Think "Less Is More"

The less-is-more mantra is another thing to look at it in a fresh way. It turns out that less is more for your brain as well as for your waistline and overall health. Eating, digesting, and eliminating any food—particularly sweets, white flour, and fat—take a toll on your brain. That's because these foods produce high rates of tissue-damaging free radicals, and as the most porous organ in your body, your brain is particularly vulnerable to free radical damage.

Overeating also damages your brain through your heart. Excess energy burdens your cardiovascular system, which in turn narrows blood vessels, thus limiting blood flow. Once again, your brain bears the brunt of this, because it is the most oxygen-dependent organ in your entire body. Keep in mind that eating slightly less than the amount you need to carry out your vital functions or keep healthy and alive has been shown to boost immunity, reduce the debilitating effects of aging, and reduce the risk of some illnesses. In one of our studies, we found that ingesting fewer calories lessened colorectal tumors in rats.

Undereating, or hypocaloric eating, (I call it "ascetic eating")—with its emphasis on fresh foods, eating slightly less than required, and weighing slightly below normal weight—reduces tissue damage and prolongs youthfulness and longevity. Yes, it may take years of transitioning to be able to eat this way, and admittedly, it is not for everyone. Moreover, it is certainly not necessary for weight loss. But it's important to recognize how far the power of ascetic eating can take you. And while it may take decades of eating evolution to progress to this point, once there, this kind of eating is reported to be effortless. Whether you decide to move toward such a goal is up to you.

Be Aware That Fat-Free Is Not Calorie-Free

As you begin to change your eating habits, keep in mind the counterintuitive fact that an absence of fat does not mean an absence of calories. In fact, according to researchers, you tend to ingest 28 percent more calories when eating low-fat foods because you overestimate the calorie savings. The visceral brain takes over and tries to win out over the reflective brain by saying in effect, "I want it and it's not so bad. After all, it's low fat!" The reflective brain lets down its guard, and off you go.

Keep Fresh Fruit on the Kitchen Counter

Whether you're at home or even on vacation, keeping fresh fruit visible makes it more accessible and a more likely snack choice. Now that you know it works that way, however, try to keep your guard up and not be swayed by the low-fat fantasy.

Use the Third Person

Odd as it may sound, research has shown that adopting the third-person perspective about yourself helps you move toward self-improvement. That makes the third-person perspective an exceptionally good motivational tool. Instead of thinking of yourself as "I," adopt the practice of referring to yourself as "she" or "he." Tell yourself that [your name] is trying hard to cut back on portion size, is doing a fine job retraining her brain, or seems to be losing weight.

Treat Yourself

Another important tip for making progress is to ensure that you do at least one thing each day that gives you pleasure. The reason, of course, is that you tend to overeat when life's pleasures are scarce; your brain substitutes one need for another and uses food to "solve" dissatisfaction. By giving yourself a bit of pleasure each day, you reduce the chance that your brain will need to send you into feeding mode to achieve a feeling of contentment.

The OPT Program's Eating Neuroregulation Tools

As you did with the regulation tools in Chapter 5, focus on a new eating tool each day so that you gradually incorporate new eating strategies into your lifestyle. All of these tools will help you gain control of your negative habits, and some will even target the part of your eating brain that caused your wobble.

Day 1
The Power of Now

Lowers emotional-brain, bottom-up influence and strengthens top-down reasoning

While anticipation and curiosity can be effective mechanisms for measuring program progress and adjusting accordingly (see Day 6 for a complete explanation), nothing is as powerful to the brain as right now. This very moment trumps past experience and future possibilities. In fact, now is so powerful that the brain tends to confuse it with what will happen at a later time. It projects what it feels right now, in passing, as a future reality ("I am miserable now, and I see no end in sight to my misery," or "I am so stuffed from this huge meal that I will never eat again."). In other words, the power of now is so great that we form future impressions based on what our senses and bodily states tell us in the present.

The Science. Studies have shown that when we anticipate eating less food at a future time, our expectation of whether that will be comfortable or uncomfortable is the present. If we're uncomfortable, we anticipate discomfort from eating less; if we're comfortable when we anticipate that future of less food, we'll expect to feel comfortable with it when it happens.

One study asked participants to estimate how much food they would be eating the following week. People who had just eaten underestimated the amount, while those who were hungry overestimated it. In another study, people were asked what they would miss first if they washed up on a deserted island. Hungry people said they would miss food first. Those who were thirsty when answering the question were sure they would miss water. Therefore, the way we feel at the moment we are asked to project our future reactions wins out over any logical consideration. (Logically, the body is in greater danger from dehydration than from starvation.) Even the ability to imagine the future can be overruled by the power of now.

Using the Power. Obviously, your current emotional state can wreak havoc with your ability to judge accurately and realistically whether you have lost or gained weight, eaten too much, or exercised too little. In those cases, you want to minimize the power of now, primarily by being aware of it.

But you can use the power in a proactive sense as well, particularly when starting a weight-loss plan or confronting setbacks that you want to reverse. You'll want to start your plan on a day when your senses and bodily state are comfortable, when you've had a restful night's sleep, feel good about yourself, have eaten healthfully, and are feeling satisfied and not deprived of food. You also don't want to be facing acute physical or emotional concerns. When your current reality is optimistic in general, you will also be optimistic about your ability to manage your eating.

The same is true if you are restarting your weight-loss plan. Choose a day when you feel comfortable with yourself and can see yourself feeling comfortable in the future. On such a day, the power of now should be sufficient to keep your brain reflective, thinking in a top-down way, able to see that "this too shall pass," and that the future can be even better than the present.

Day 2
Go Green and Avoid the Gray Zone

Helps strengthen the brain brake and diffuses tugs from the emotional brain

I call it the "green zone." It's the time after a meal when you are completely satisfied and free of food longings; you're not stuffed, but you're certainly not hungry, and food does not show up anywhere on your radar screen. The green zone is a liberating place to be, but it's hard to stay there.

The gray zone is something else altogether. It's the mental and physical space in which you are biologically indifferent to food. You're neither hungry nor satisfied. You could eat if you saw something you liked, if the friend you're with were eating, or if your child wanted something. Otherwise, you would pass.

Scientific evidence is clear that eating in the gray zone is what accounts for today's obesity epidemic. If you were to assign numbers to the urge for eating, with one representing feeling pleasantly satisfied with no urge to eat and five representing feeling famished, the gray zone would be the scores from two to four. You can find yourself in the gray zone less than an hour after a meal, even though physiologically you are not likely to be hungry—or to need food—for at least two and a half hours after eating. The gray zone, however, is limbo; you could go either way.

The Science. Scientists call the phenomenon of the gray zone "metabolic indifference." Physical indicators of hunger—glucose, insulin, stomach stress receptors—are not signaling hunger, yet your eating brain's satiety switch is still not on. So you're not hungry, but you're not satisfied, either.

This state of metabolic indifference happens to be where most of us in the Western world find ourselves, and this is precisely the state in which we do most of our nibbling, foraging for something that's within easy reach. Of course, if your brain is in this state and food is around, the mirroring process will push you over the edge, and you will eat that food.

Green Eating. This tool teaches you to beat limbo, to stay in the green zone for as long as you can and, above all, to avoid the gray zone. Start by setting a feeding schedule, just as you might for an infant. But in this case, the main aim is to declare specific food-free time between meals and snacks.

Okay, what if it turns out that you find it difficult to wait at least two and a half hours between meals? What do you do? First, work up to the two-and-a-half-hour goal in increments. Start with a time of twenty-five minutes, then forty-five minutes, an hour, and gradually increase the wait to two and a half hours. Once you've got that nailed, wait three hours or even four. If your eating brain signals for food during one of these waiting times, remind yourself that you don't need it. Tell yourself, "I am in the green zone, free of food for the next [however many] hours."

When you find yourself thinking of food, rate your hunger on a scale of one to five and try to distinguish between a desire or craving and real hunger. Try to figure out what you are really hungry for. After all, if you just ate an hour ago, you don't need food. Tell yourself you are not really hungry and that food is not what you want. Ask yourself what you *do* want. Consider how staying in the green zone frees you from all the constraints of the eating scene, offering a time-out from thinking about food, preparing food, eating, digesting, and cleaning up.

Sometimes the urge to eat may be too great. Try to satisfy it with a mint or sugarless gum. If you absolutely cannot wait, choose a high-fiber snack; it will keep you busy preparing and chewing, and fiber helps you feel full. Try a handful of shelled pistachio nuts or almonds, or an orange.

There are even some tricks you can play on your eating brain. Purse your lips or lightly bring them together to signal your eating brain that this door is closed. Then press your palm against your belly to reinforce the connection between your desire to eat and the fact that your body has had enough. The pressure of your open palm on your stomach may be the reassurance you are after.

If you can't stop thinking of food, the best solution is distraction or escape. Getting yourself away from accessible food may not be easy, but it can be the only way to prevent unwanted eating.

Above all, keep in mind that you are in the limbo of the gray zone. The more you recognize it for what it is, the easier it becomes to go green.

Day 3
Fool Your Brain

Tricks the emotional brain so you eat less

Put "portion distortion" to work for you. Since the brain has no objective way of knowing exactly how much you are eating, it relies on soft cues. It follows a simple rule and tells you to eat pretty much all of the total quantity in front of you. So limit the quantity of food in front of you; if you have eight chicken wings at your disposal, choose six or four or two for your plate.

The brain judges quantity by scanning the top or rim of a serving dish. If there is a lot of empty space, it feels short-changed, so it will feel justified in sending you back for seconds or looking for something more to eat. That's what happens if you put eight ounces of ice cream in a bowl that could hold sixteen ounces. You eat the eight ounces and think you still want more. If, on the other hand, the ice cream is heaped high above the rim of the dish, your brain is satisfied that it's getting a fair deal.

The Science. Over the past two decades, the typical portion size of many of the foods and beverages we consume in the United States has increased by 20 percent to more than 100 percent as is the case for orange juice. This amounts to taking in five more pounds of food per year just by drinking the typical oversized portion of orange juice. When you add up the 135 percent increase in calories in soft drinks, megabowls of pasta, and fast-food meals, you can see how easy the energy surplus adds up.

We eat more when we're given more, we're influenced to eat more by the size of the package portion, and we tend not to compensate for eating too much at one sitting by eating less at the next. A famous 2002 study gave fifty-one people four different portion sizes of macaroni and cheese on different days. The bigger the portion size, the more people ate—30 percent more calories in the biggest serving compared with the smallest. The investigators also asked participants to rate their feelings of hunger and fullness after the meals. No matter what portion size participants ate, their ratings were similar, suggesting that people adjust or mask their natural feeling of fullness to accommodate greater food availability.

Another study, this one published in May 2006, focused on reactions to whether a food serving was overfilled or underfilled. Overfilling evoked positive feelings, while underfilling evoked negative feelings, and these feelings dictated people's evaluations.

Serve Smart. Let your cup runneth over. Use small-serving containers to dish up your foods and beverages, and go over the top. In other words, put your eight ounces of ice cream in a bowl that should only hold six ounces.

The reality is that you will be just as satisfied with eight ounces of ice cream as you would with sixteen. Really. Bigger only means that we eat more, not that we are more satisfied. As long as a sixteen-ounce serving is in front of you, you won't turn it down. What's a brain to do? Use your top-down thinking to override your bottom-up desires by squeezing eight ounces into a six-ounce dish so it looks like a gargantuan portion.

The same reasoning is why it helps to purchase items in small packages and avoid the "family size" of anything. Be aware that individually packaged snacks are not necessarily individual servings. A single muffin can be four servings of 180 calories each. Yet since it's packaged individually, you may not feel full until you've eaten the whole thing. If you do, make a conscious note that you are "in debt" and have to repay it by eating less next time.

And keep in mind that food manufacturers profit from your false belief that bigger is better by offering megaportions for a token additional fee. Adding extra ounces of food is the cheapest way for the food vendor to shift your bottom-up, more-is-better thinking into overdrive. Top-down thinking is your friend. It says, "More can kill you," and it's right.

Add to top-down decision making by letting the "evidence" of your eating pile up: a glance at the wastebasket, kitchen counter, or kitchen sink can be a powerful reminder of what you ate earlier on. Your brain is given another opportunity to remind your stomach that it's had enough.

Day 4
Avoid Appetizers

Inhibits the limbic system's bottom-up influence

There is a reason appetizers come in combination platters. Think of a wonderful platter of Italian antipasto. Each food tantalizes and stimulates a particular taste: savory, fat, crunchy, salty. By the time you finish with the appetizer plate, your taste buds are dancing. And your appetite soars! That's the point: appetizers are meant to promote eating.

The Science. Sampling a wide variety of tastes and textures stimulates the appetite. It's easier to pass on a food altogether than to "eat just one." No matter how sincere your intention to have a little taste, the merest morsel can make your brain eager for more, and you know by now that the brain wins.

Scientists tell us there are two ways we feel satisfaction from eating—by the amount we eat and by taste. They call the latter "taste satiety," which refers to the fact that you can be completely satisfied after a meal of chicken and field greens, but your taste for a burger is still there. You are full, true enough, but not too full for that burger.

It is also true that the more flavors you have available, the more you tend to eat. Animals eat basically the same foods every day, and they are amazingly healthy. The drive to eat is stimulated by the expectation of food because the first bite—or even the possibility of eating—triggers the release of appetite-stimulating chemicals known as orexigenic peptides. Start eating and you switch on the hunger circuits, a phenomenon that researcher Gareth Long calls "the appetizing effect of food itself."

Become Anti-app. The solution is simply to avoid variety. Avoid sampling. Instead, choose one healthy representative of each food group. For example, have grilled chicken or a turkey burger or steak as a protein option. When choosing a starch, pick one—such as whole-wheat bread, a roll, or a slice of crusty Italian bread—but not a sampling of each. Limit the *range* of what you taste.

This is not to be confused with contradicting the nutritionist mantra to eat from all food groups. Certainly, you want to eat a protein, a complex carbohydrate, and a vegetable with just about every meal.

Rather, the variety I am asking you to avoid is the sampling of a little bit—and often a lot—of everything in front of you: steak, chicken, hot dogs, french fries, baked potatoes, potato salad, pasta, rice, cheesecake, éclairs, and cake. You get the picture.

Day 5
Think for Yourself

Strengthens the inquisitive, "just the facts" frontal area and boosts the reflective brain's top-down influence

The brain wants to believe what it reads and hears. If the menu in the fast-food restaurant says that the fried chicken meal is "part of a healthy lifestyle," the brain accepts it. For one thing, if it weren't true, it wouldn't be right there on the menu for everyone to see, right? And for another, we would really like to believe that fried chicken is healthy. No wonder a small sign with the word *healthy* can toss our top-down thinking out the window. A fried chicken dinner it is!

The Science. The brain's design leads to known computational errors. Some of these errors are the direct result of the difference between the world in which the human brain evolved and the world we live in today. For instance, the brain's tendency to accept "facts" presented by others was a useful tool in prehistoric times. Back then, if someone in the group shouted, "T-Rex! Run," those who ran had a better chance of surviving than those who waited around to find out for themselves if the statement was correct. We're all descendants of those survivors, but today, their leftover tendency can lead us to accept claims that are not true. It's a kind of cognitive miserliness; we just let others do our thinking and save ourselves the effort.

There is evidence that overweight people might be even more susceptible to this problem. After all, if you are overweight, your body keeps telling you to eat nonstop, and you know that can't be right. The disconnect seems to be proof that your body can't be trusted. This may make you especially vulnerable to weight-loss scams and may help explain the puzzling finding that the weight-loss industry has the highest rate of return customers. Put another way, this industry has the lowest rate of success in delivering the results its customers have paid for.

In addition to its tendency to follow others' thinking, the brain can also fall prey to a cognitive dissonance that misleads us into accepting food facts that are obviously wrong. The idea of cognitive dissonance is based on the fact that we are inherently designed to look for ways to reduce internal conflict and turmoil. A fried chicken dinner is desirable but conflicts with what our doctors and our own common sense have told us is healthy. How do we reduce the inner tension? Simple. We build up the benefits of eating the fried chicken dinner or diminish the risks. Reading the sign that claims fried chicken is healthy helps to diminish the risk. Listening to our visceral mind's craving for the taste of fried chicken, supported by a million foodscape cues, builds up its benefits. Temporarily at least, we soothe our cognitive dissonance by eating the fried chicken. It's only later, when our top-down thinking mind kicks in again, that regret sets in, bringing its own form of cognitive dissonance.

Why are we such easy targets? After all, most of us know what's healthy and what's not. In my view, we are gullible because it feels so good to believe the false claim—"It's good for me to eat chocolate because it has chemicals that work like antidepressants." These words help us throw caution to the wind, forget the calories, and open the floodgates to chocoholic indulgence. If it didn't feel so good to believe that the false is truth, we would most likely judge the chocolate to be against our own best interest.

The food industry is heavily invested in getting us to consume food excessively, especially the high-calorie stuff that is so very profitable. They have taken their fight for your dollar right into your brain, trying to exploit its vulnerabilities—like cognitive miserliness and cognitive dissonance—to increase sales. To avoid being collateral damage in this battle, use your brain at its best to think for yourself how to achieve healthy living and weight loss.

Think Yourself Thin. You know better, and to lose weight, you really have to act on what you know. You need to use the thinking part of your brain, the part that has absorbed knowledge, questions claims, and sifts through opposing arguments to arrive at a sensible course of action.

For example, you know that losing weight means eating less food and burning more calories. Ads that claim you can eat all you want of some food or other or that you can eat any food you choose are likely to be based on no or shabby scientific research. In fact, if you find yourself focusing on eating more of any food—even fiber or other healthy choices—as a way to lose weight, that's a telltale sign that you are still struggling with the idea of eating less. Go back to some of the regulation tools like mirroring, MIPs, rebooting, and the brain brake till your brain can achieve a paradigm shift. Permanent weight loss means being comfortable when you eat less. Period.

The truth is that there is ample information available on which you can base your eating choices. Armed with this information, you can avoid the nutritional pitfall of equating any healthy food with an opportunity for weight loss. Yes, almonds are great for your heart, oatmeal reduces cholesterol, and orange juice is full of vitamins and antioxidants. But these healthy foods are also highly caloric. So weigh the nutritional facts against the weight-gain facts, and judge accordingly.

The nutritional labels on food packages are a veritable treasure trove of information. As you approach that muffin or fruit pie for your midmorning snack, take time to read the label. You may be stunned to learn that each item delivers a hefty 750 calories, about 350 of them from fat. Since you've already had breakfast, this snack is not an essential; it's an elective. Are you prepared to expend that many calories on a mere snack? If you're counting calories—and weight loss is all about calories—that will mean eating very, very little for the rest of the day. Can you manage that? If you decide you can "burn it off," be aware of what that means; in the case of 750 calories, you would need to walk up about 275 flights of stairs, jump rope for an hour, or walk very briskly for at least two hours.

Using your brain to lose weight also means choosing a weight-loss plan based on your own particular overeating pitfalls. Just because Mary Jane lost twenty-four pounds eating a dozen small meals a day doesn't mean you will. As noted earlier in this book, there are plenty of sound, sensible weight-loss plans out there. The key to making any plan work is to find your level of comfort. Whether your problem is limiting portions, stopping eating once you get started, or being reluctant to exercise, there is no doubt a plan will work for you once your brain can self-regulate.

Day 6
Set Clear Goals, Measure, and Adjust

Strengthens the frontal lobes and prefrontal cortexes, strengthens the brain brake, and encourages top-down actions

How much do you want to weigh? How many pounds a week should you lose? What should your estimated daily caloric intake be to achieve your desired weight loss? Losing weight and managing a healthy weight are a matter of setting clear goals and measuring progress toward (or away from) them, then adjusting your behavior to get back on track.

The more wishy-washy you are about your eating and weight goals, the more likely you are to resign yourself to slipups, reverses, weight gain, and poor eating. Only by setting clear goals, monitoring your progress, and taking steps to adjust your program when you're not meeting those goals can you accomplish what you want to do.

The Science. Anticipation and curiosity are the reasons measuring helps you lose weight. Study volunteers who were asked to choose between a candy bar and finding out the answers to a quiz before taking the quiz chose the candy bar, hands down. When given the same choice after taking the quiz, however, the choice was overwhelmingly in favor of knowing the test results. The candy bar lost out to curiosity the second time because the volunteers were anticipating feedback information at that point. When you're curious about your next weigh-in and you anticipate that the number will please you, it can motivate you to let go of a treat that's being offered.

There's a science of anticipation. In his book, *Sweet Anticipation,* David Huron writes of the brain mechanisms that physically and emotionally ready the body to tolerate cutbacks in eating. Anticipating a weigh-in triggers the body's defensive response system, which puts it on alert. This state of alertness demands more energy and thus boosts metabolism, using more calories. It also translates to heightened sensory responses, which make us more aware of the taste and amount of food we eat. At the same time, the state of uncertainty about our weight creates some tension, but unlike distress, it is what Huron calls "eustress"—temporary, mild, controllable, and created not by adversity but by curiosity and looking forward to something good. This also means heightened awareness and higher calorie expenditure. So we burn more calories, and we become better at tracking our eating and weight.

Anticipating weigh-ins also engages our cognitive anticipatory system that rewards us when we can predict our weight accurately, offering an additional incentive to lose more. In addition, imagination kicks into this process. If we can imagine the happiness of weight loss, we can combat the urge to eat that second bowl of cereal or the sugary dessert; in other words, imagination boosts the brain brake's ability to delay gratification. Finally, anticipating the weigh-in energizes our appraisal mechanism as we wonder how we're doing on our weight-loss program. This is exactly the type of reflective-brain, top-down thinking that's vital to weight loss.

The science of biofeedback plays a role in weight-loss goal setting because it teaches us about adjusting our actions. Studies show that dieters who took biofeedback-like steps to correct setbacks in their weight-loss programs were more successful than dieters who were simply aware that they were regaining weight but did not take corrective action. Taking quick steps to reverse the setbacks meant that the dieters using biofeedback were 82 percent less likely to regain five or more pounds, as dieters typically do.

Science also shows us why it's important to have no regrets. Making a catastrophe out of yet another setback drains energy and leads to chaos and disorganization. A healthy response to a setback is to find a clear solution; that way, you regain control and self-regulation. Too often when you blow your diet, it becomes an excuse to continue the failure ("The day is shot, so I might as well eat everything I want."). No regrets means that you start over instead of giving in to that negative thinking.

Setting Stellar Goals. The tools for measuring are a scale, the way your clothes feel, the way you feel about yourself, and daily records of your eating and exercise. All are worthwhile. The goals you set, however, come first, for they are what you are measuring yourself against.

Set a goal for the weight and, if applicable, the level of physical fitness you want to attain. Then set interim goals that define your plan to achieve your goal weight and fitness—that is, the number of pounds you should safely lose each week, the number of calories you will be able to eat per day, what types of exercise you will need to do for how long, and so on. Decide also what you are willing to accept as a healthy eating day.

Then weigh yourself daily or every couple of days. Observe if your clothes feel tighter or looser. Scrutinize your eating and exercise logs every day. Adjust as you must. If you are overeating, gaining weight, or failing to lose weight, change your program. You might reduce calories by a third, double your physical activity, or both until your weight is where you want it. Determine the reasons for your weight gain or lack of progress. Is it a matter of portion size? Frequency of eating? Food choices? Find the cause and take action to change the results.

Above all, have no regrets. Avoid getting emotional about a lack of progress or setbacks. Instead, turn your energy to the immediate future and decide what you can do this moment, for the rest of the day, and for the remainder of the week to compensate. Look to your regulation tools to help you reverse the situation.

Day 7
Give Yourself a Sugar High

Offsets the body's stress response and protects against limbic system overactivity

Sugar can take the edge off the toxic effects of stress on the body. I'm talking about *real* sugar.

Am I honestly suggesting you have a cookie, piece of cake, or chocolate bar as part of retraining your brain for weight loss? Yes. Sweets made of real sugar—and only those made of real sugar—are effective in combating the adverse effects of stress, and stress, as you know, triggers numerous neurochemical and hormonal changes that harm your physical and psychological health and lead to weight gain.

The Science. Think of it in terms of cost versus benefit. Yes, sugar can play havoc with your blood glucose level, is high in nonnutritious calories, and ruins your teeth. That's the cost. But there is also a cost exacted by stress, which can take a terrible toll on the body. So in times of stress—if you are going through a particularly rough time at home, are working long hours, have suffered a traumatic event, aren't sleeping well, are in the midst of a crisis in your relationship, or just feel that your mind and body are taking a beating—eating sweets can be beneficial.

Specifically, the sugar counteracts hormones and chemicals that have a negative effect on your body and weight—the glucocorticoids, epinephrine, and norepinephrine released by stress triggers. Cortisol, for example, is a glucocorticoid to which your body reacts by turning up fat formation and deposition, especially around your waist.

Stress is also a factor in behavioral changes that adversely affect your weight. You get to the point where you simply don't care enough about your wellness to eat healthfully. It's a vicious cycle: stress makes you neglect self-care, which creates more stress, and so on.

Add Sweetness to Your Life. What's the best way to get your "hit" of sweetness? One method is to opt for sugar without the fat—jelly beans, licorice sticks, or hard candy. Another is to take your sweetness the natural way from dried fruit like dates or raisins, or fresh fruit topped with cinnamon, maple syrup, or honey.

Weigh the costs of stress against the calorie cost of a sugar-based sweet, and weigh the benefit to be realized from those feel-good neurochemicals sugar produces in your brain. If it computes well for overall weight loss, by all means, go for the sugar treat.

Day 8
Reward Yourself Wisely

Helps build healthy eating memories and promotes neurochemicals that stimulate healthy choices

We almost can't help using food as a reward or compensation when we're low. The trick is to use it in the direction of weight loss.

First, use comfort food as a pat on the back rather than as a life vest. Reward yourself with food for your successes, rather than using it to stay afloat. Eat your favorite sweet or fatty meal on a Good Day!

Second, redefine comfort food as healthful foods, not the high-calorie "treats" you usually think of when you use the term.

When your self-esteem is at rock bottom, don't reward yourself with comfort food, lift it with fresh vegetables and fruits beautifully presented on special dinnerware. Light some candles. Eat to the sounds of your favorite music. You'll feel better about yourself while you're eating, and you'll take special comfort in knowing that you did not veer from your healthy weight-loss plan.

The Science. Studies have shown that men reward themselves for their successes with healthy food, while women comfort themselves with fatty sweets when they meet with failure. The laws of conditioning are clear, however, that if you reward failure with a rich treat, you will just keep failing so you can get the prize. Besides, all too often, food is used as comfort for having failed at weight loss.

Positive feelings trigger healthier eating than do negative emotions. When you feel at the top of your game, you are likely to select carbohydrate- and protein-rich meals. Conversely, emotional bumps trigger cravings for high-calorie foods that rewire your eating brain: the more of them you eat, the more you want to eat. These foods, of course, also add more calories ounce for ounce than protein.

In addition, when you eat to quell unhappiness, you become behaviorally conditioned to using food as solace to the point that the slightest hint of an emotional setback provokes eating.

Redefining Comfort. Condition yourself the other way. Your brain can establish a pattern of rewarding your wellness with healthy foods instead of your failures with fatty sweets. Teach yourself to take comfort in success by choosing healthy eating as a reward for feeling good about yourself.

Day 9
Turn On the Heat

Facilitates a feeling of satisfaction and fullness by turning off the eating switch in the hypothalamus earlier so you eat less

When it comes to eating satisfaction, a hot calorie is worth more than a cold one.

The Science. The reason warm food is more satisfying than cold is that the machinery inside the hypothalamus that regulates the on/off eating switch is right next to the controls for temperature regulation. Scientists believe that under some circumstances, neighboring locations can excite each other by crossing signals across shared borders.

Indeed, hunger and cold are intimately related at the core of our genetic inheritance. The spillover effect is not great; we still know when we are just hungry or just cold. But, as you may have experienced firsthand, being hungry often means being more sensitive to cold. There's a sound evolutionary reason for this: when the ambient temperature drops consistently, it triggers the body to prepare for a long, hard winter ahead. That means the body goes into energy-preservation mode, eating high-energy foods and depositing a greater proportion of calories as fat. In fact, that's why winter weight gain is so common; it's the spillover in brain real estate across shared anatomical borders.

Eat Hot. Whenever possible, choose hot foods over cold—the warm grilled chicken over chicken salad, hot oatmeal over cold bran flakes, hot pasta over cold pasta salad. The one exception to this is the green salad; it satisfies not just through taste, but because it requires more chewing and takes up more stomach space. But otherwise, when your food gets cold, reheat it or toss it in favor of another hot dish that will leave you feeling comfortable and satisfied.

Day 10
Chew Your Calories

Leads to stronger signals from the gastrointestinal tract to the hypothalamus, and lets the hypothalamus know when you have had enough nourishment

Chew more to ingest fewer calories. From fruits and vegetables to fish and meats to candy and sweets, when you are looking for something to eat, consider the chewing factor: the longer you chew your food, the longer the eating satisfaction and the more full you will feel.

The Science. We humans didn't always cook the foods we ate, but switching to cooked foods allowed us to eat about 2,000 calories per hour compared to the 400 calories per hour our ancestors got from chewing and swallowing uncooked game.

The diminished need for chewing with cooked foods has actually changed the shape of the human skull, making it about 12 percent smaller than it was in the Paleolithic era some two million years ago. But chew on this: in a few months of vigorous chewing that strengthens those muscles around your mouth, you can actually add dimension to your lower face, helping you get that stronger, firmer chin you've always wanted. The opposite is also true, at least for pigs: in a matter of months, pigs fed a diet of softened food developed shorter and narrower snouts than those who received a hard-food diet.

Do you suppose that a calorie is a calorie whether it comes from protein, carbohydrate, or fat, and that it makes no difference whether you drink it, slurp it, or chew it? Turns out that it takes less energy to convert fat calories into fat than protein calories, so the fattier the food, the greater the fat deposit.

As for drinking your calories, consider that just one sugar-sweetened soft drink per day multiplies the risk of obesity 1.6 times. Moreover, liquid calories bypass your brain's watchful eye, skipping right past its satiety signals, so they don't really register—except in adding inches to your waistline. These drinks glide through your intestinal tract without triggering your brain's calorie-tracking system. Since your brain doesn't know that you just took in 400 calories, it doesn't tell you when you've had enough.

Just Chew It. Think of food as a vehicle for delivering energy in the form of calories and nutrients. Quickly ingested foods deliver the goods fast and cheap, while foods you chew for a long time and ingest slowly deliver substantive satisfaction.

Therefore, choose foods you can chew in place of soft, palatable foods like mashed potatoes and gravy, white bread and peanut butter, and processed fatty meats. Instead, go for tougher, more satisfying options like raw vegetables, nuts, fruits, field greens, whole grains, and lean, unprocessed meats. Raw foods, like crudités, give you chewing satisfaction and have other advantages as well. They contain more fiber, take more time to be turned into usable energy, are more filling, and take longer to process through the intestinal tract, thus leaving you feeling full for a long while.

Last Thoughts and Helpful Hints

Well done! You are among the first to make changes in your eating easier by retraining your brain and optimizing its performance. As you've figured out by now, the retrain-your-brain concept relies mostly on your brain to do the work needed for weight management. No longer are you fighting yourself to do the right thing. Your brain enables you to follow a healthy diet. When self-defeating behaviors like overeating are left up to you to control—the "just stop it" strategy—the results are usually bleak. That's because the "you" in charge of this strategy is made up of different areas of your brain that are all pulling in different directions.

The point is the less you rely on self-control to manage your weight, the greater your chance of success. The OPT program bypasses the willpower step by not pitting you against your nature but rather using your nature—your brain—to work for you. Your cooperation is most important in the first part of the program: simply try out the actions and experiences in the program as described. Once you expose your brain to these experiences, it will take over part of the process. It will rearrange itself so it doesn't call on you as often or as loudly to deliver the yummies—foods that trigger the feel-good chemicals that it thinks are so great for you. In other words, your desire for food will lessen, making it easier for you to eat in the way you choose (top-down, reflective-brain, balanced eating).

The first step, implementation—actually making a point to follow the tools—is both the strongest and the weakest link of this whole process. Strong because your mighty brain is on your side, and weak because (you guessed it) your mighty brain is on your side.

Your strength as a human being rests partly with the fact that you can make a decision at this moment or anytime to change something, anything about your behavior and then proceed to do it. Ironically this "gift" is also a downfall: you can choose to forget the whole thing and go back to your old ways of eating and living.

> The less you rely on self-control to manage your weight, the greater your chance of success.

But something tells me that now that you've learned about the mechanisms that truly control your eating, your views about how to manage your weight will be irreversibly changed. Now that you know that unhealthy eating is a method for delivering neurochemicals or balance to soothe your powerful, craving brain, your eating and weight-loss approaches are bound to be affected. No matter what happens next, even if you don't consciously implement a single tool, since your perceptions of weight gain and weight loss are changed, your eating behavior will change automatically. If the data and explanations for weight gain make sense to you now, it's almost impossible for you to go backward; it's like once you have experienced electricity, going back to candle-light and pretending that electricity doesn't exist is impossible.

Once you reframe your unhealthy eating, see it from this new angle, and repeat the OPT actions, you begin traveling down the path of self-driven process. Your brain takes over, and as it becomes healthier and more robust, it no longer needs the fix that unhealthy foods deliver. Make no mistake. You eat these foods because you crave them, or are addicted to them, but you have a second, hidden addiction going on inside your brain that you probably haven't thought about—an addiction to dopamine, serotonin, and endorphine.

After implementing the OPT tools, you must make them a part of your life. That's a step that your brain will take for you. Just by using the tools as recommended, your brain will respond to their effects, even if you don't notice them. Since the tools are helpful to your brain, helping it to regulate itself better, it will opt for more. This means that you will find it easier and easier to use the OPT actions. Since repetitions build neural highways, before you know it, these behaviors and habits will become second nature to you. They move to the "automatic" mode in your brain; there's no need to consciously plan to use them.

"Show the brain a better way of doing things and it catches on quickly" was how my colleague Dan McDonnell explained the self-driven improvement in brain function after being "treated" with the neurofeedback procedure. Neurofeedback is a method for balancing the brain. It uses an electroencephalograph to boost brain fitness by changing brainwave activity patterns. A study that followed people three years after retraining with neurofeedback showed that the brain not only kept the improved patterns, but continued to improve on its own. The OPT program aims to do the same thing without the use of instruments.

Cures for Slipups

The best way to maintain what you have learned from the program is to use the tools long enough for your brain to take over.

Setbacks do happen even to the fittest among us. "You'd better tell us what to do when we slip up. That's the most important problem for many of us," one young woman lamented even before she started the program. I have found that overeaters tend to be particularly troubled and jarred by one day's unhealthy eating. Understandably, they fear regressing—going back to their old ways—to the point of panic. As you might expect, panic exaggerates the initial reason you overate in the first place, and before you know it, weight management is out the window. A slipup is not the end of the world—just focus on how you will make it up the next time!

Should you have a slipup, reboot your system, shifting to self-maintenance with regulation tools such as body pleasure, feeding your mind, and mindfulness. Problem eating is your red flag to take care of yourself; it means you ignored the warning signs that came a few days before. In time, you will be able to see a slipup coming, because it will be foretold by poor sleep, a bad mood, and general discomfort. That is the ideal time for proactive intervention: soothe yourself by feeding your senses and being mindful when you see the danger on the horizon.

Use each tool as described and return to the tool(s) you sense will give you what you want to soothe a particular discomfort. As a rule, body pleasure, mindfulness, and feeding your mind are good tools to help you regain the interest and motivation to live healthier. The more pleasure you give yourself, the more self-accepting you are, the more likely you will be to find you are worth the investment to attain a healthy weight.

Rewire Your Brain with Food

Finally, a key step in retraining your brain to lose weight is diet. Many of the people who have entered the OPT program have used diets that limit calories but neglect brain health. The BrainMed Diet described in Chapter 7 was developed to address the gap between a healthy diet and a brain-boosting healthy diet. The BrainMed program reflects my blended roots. As a Greek, I included Mediterranean foods recognized for their positive effects on health and longevity. As an American, I sought simplicity and ease of preparation. The result is a blend of brain-healthy Mediterranean-style foods that are simple and easy to prepare. Going a step further, BrainMed foods have been selected to rewire your DNA in a positive direction. In Chapter 2, we discussed the field of nutrigenomics, specifically the process whereby unhealthy foods rewire genes to behave differently, most often leading to metabolic disorders and chronic medical conditions.

The BrainMed foods, style, and methods of preparation are also designed to effect changes in your genetic makeup, but in a positive manner, by turning genes on or off and altering hormone levels to bring your body and mind closer to optimal health.

The BrainMed Diet

Eating the Mediterranean Way

Taking any meal and adding a few crumbs of feta and olives has, unhappily, come to translate to "Mediterranean cuisine." However, cooking Mediterranean is far more complex and usually foods are cooked slowly. The Mediterranean-style foods included in the BrainMed Diet have been selected for taste, brain benefit, and simplicity of preparation.

While this is not a diet book, the BrainMed Diet plan is a snapshot of the type of eating to strive for. Before you reach for the predictable panic button ("What's left to eat?"), remember the universal rule: profound events and changes seem profound because you see them as finished products. The human brain, for instance, has taken millions of years of constant, small adjustments to evolve to its present level of complexity. Take away the element of gradual change in response to environmental demands and look only at the finished product, and the brain may seem nothing short of a miracle. The process of healthy eating also requires gradual, consistent changes all geared toward a single goal: weight management. Healthy eating, like any evolution and progress, is a matter of slow changes over time. The key is to change in the desired direction.

The BrainMed Diet will feed both your brain and your body. Use it as a guide to help you determine what truly healthy eating is and to gauge your own progress on an hourly and daily basis.

Why Mediterranean?

The benefits of Mediterranean cooking have been known for fifty years; however, scientists are continuing to discover the exact reasons for those benefits. What about these foods and associated methods of eating and cooking are beneficial?

First, Mediterranean cooking places more emphasis on fruits, vegetables, fish, and olive oil and less emphasis on meats and refined convenience foods. Fruits include citrus—such as oranges and tangerines—as well as apples, peaches, apricots, grapes, melons, and pears. Vegetables are the basic staple and the chief ingredient in every meal. Often, fresh vegetables are eaten as snacks—much as we may use fruit in the United States. Tomatoes, green beans, peppers, and cucumbers are often enjoyed au naturale—raw and without seasoning. Because meats are not necessarily eaten daily, the source of almost all fat is derived from a healthier source: olive oil.

Serving portions of meats, fruits, and vegetables may be dramatically different from what you're accustomed to. For example, vegetables are supersized, while meats are served in small, modest amounts. Visiting the local agora, or public fruit and vegetable market, in my home city of Nafplion, I am shocked at the quantities the natives find "average." Potatoes, legumes, lettuce, celery, cauliflower, or carrots are bought in large quantities of six to eight pounds. Twelve pounds of apricots, a dozen cucumbers, eight pounds of grapes, purchased at least twice a week, especially when in season, are part of a typical grocery list for an average family.

These amounts make sense when you consider that the typical Mediterranean meal is almost always accompanied by a salad and may be served with three or more side dishes of vegetables. As you can see, the Mediterranean diet gives *supersizing* a whole new meaning.

If you had to single out one ingredient in the Mediterranean diet as the biggest contributor to good health and longevity, it would most likely be olive oil. Although as high in calories as any other oil, it has far-reaching health benefits, from cardiovascular health to cancer protection, and even shiny hair and clear skin.

Mediterranean cooking places more emphasis on fruits, vegetables, fish, and olive oil and less emphasis on meats and refined convenience foods.

Olive oil and other basic staples like green leafy vegetables, fish, legumes, and fruit contain high amounts of antioxidants—substances shown to protect the body from free radicals, inflammation, and poor blood flow, the three major sources of injury to organs and body tissues. In addition, they are high in ingredients such as omega-3 fatty acids, vitamins, and phytochemicals that help optimize the way the body functions. Let's take a closer look at the precise mechanisms through which these foods help maintain good health and prolong longevity.

The Benefits of a Mediterranean Diet

In Chapter 4, you learned how to create a healthy environment for your brain, and in Chapters 5 and 6, you were introduced to specific brain-training exercises. Now you are about to learn even more ways to help your brain thrive, this time through a healthy diet. The Mediterranean foods included in the BrainMed Diet nourish your brain by improving blood flow, inhibiting free radicals, and easing inflammation.

Increasing Blood Flow

The brain uses up a huge proportion of the energy the body needs to stay alive. Any substance that increases blood flow throughout the body is bound to benefit the brain, delivering a steady supply of oxygen and nutrients that are essential to carry out its numerous operations. The ingredients commonly used in Mediterranean cooking—such as tomatoes, olives, fish, and olive oil—boost cardiovascular health and help blood vessels stay open and flexible, which allows a better flow of blood to the brain.

Studies have shown that replacing animal fat and oil derived from seeds with olive oil results in less damage to the walls of blood vessels. This means that if you replace all oils with olive oil, you can eat 30 percent more fat (from olive oil) without suffering the negative changes to cardiovascular function that come from other sources of fat. Keep in mind that fat, even olive oil, is still high in calories, and it increases both brain health and your waistline. So go ahead and drizzle that extra-virgin olive oil on your tomatoes, but remember you can still get too much of a good thing.

Eliminating Free Radicals

In addition to compromised blood supply, free radicals harm the brain by directly injuring nerve cells and other types of cells that are vital to processing information and strengthening the networks that link different brain areas together. Free radicals are extremely damaging to all body tissues but are especially harmful to the cells lining the cardiovascular system, nerve cells, and various brain cells.

Where do these nasty little critters come from? Believe it or not, free radicals are naturally occurring by-products of metabolism. The body uses oxygen to help break down food and turn it into energy. During this reaction, free radicals are released into the system. They are called free because they are unattached and looking for a special something to hook up with. Vulnerable tissues that make up the brain and cardiovascular system are easy prey for radical damage because they are "porous." Think of them as empathic and highly sensitive. Does that sound familiar?

What happens when something metal is left outdoors for a long time? Thanks mainly to the oxygen in the atmosphere as well as other forces, it will eventually become damaged, corroded, and rusted. Similarly, when body tissues are exposed to free radicals for long periods of time, those tissues become damaged. Eventually tissue damage, especially in vital organs like the heart or the brain, results in symptoms. Free radical damage has been implicated in cardiovascular disease, as well as dementia and other cognitive disorders.

But the body is not defenseless against these rogue terrorists. Antioxidants protect tissue from damage of any kind, including free radicals. Your body relies on the antioxidants you take in from the foods you eat to combat this damage. Mediterranean foods like leafy green vegetables, tomatoes, and fruits tend to be high in antioxidants such as vitamins A, C, and E as well as other phytochemicals and nutrients that also protect against tissue damage. Omega-3 fatty acids from fish and olive oil—basic pillars of Mediterranean cooking—are well-known brain tissue protectors. Legumes provide vital minerals as well as proteins that nourish and empower the body without generating as many tissue-damaging free radicals.

Anti-Inflammatory Agents

In addition to injury from free radicals, brain tissue is also sensitive to damage caused by inflammation. Inflammation is the body's reaction to an injury, which can range from a bee sting to eating fried chicken. Some foods are more inflammatory than others—the worst being animal fats, foods fried in fats, saturated fats, and especially trans fats. Olive oil, the most widely used fat in the Mediterranean diet, does not increase inflammation, but rather has ingredients that reduce and protect against it.

> As important as what the Mediterranean diet includes, is what it excludes or limits. For example, meat plays a less dominant role and is not offered every day or with every meal.

As important as what the Mediterranean diet includes, is what it excludes or limits. For example, meat plays a less dominant role and is not offered every day or with every meal. This restriction alone lessens the risk of injury due to inflammation, insulin irregularities, weight gain, and free radical damage, which in turn helps nurture the body and impels the brain to flourish.

What Is Mediterranean Cooking?

The following list is a snapshot of your grocery list for Mediterranean foods. These items have been selected for their low fat content and health benefits, especially to the brain.

Fruits and Vegetables

Bananas
Fresh basil
Broccoli or broccoli rabe
Carrots, stalks attached
Celery
Cucumbers
Eggplant
Fresh flowers (strictly brain food, although some, like
    pansies, are edible)
Fruit in season (large containers of oranges, pears,
    grapes, melons, berries, apples)
Garlic
Green beans
Lemons and limes
Multicolored peppers
Vidalia or sweet onions
Prewashed salad or organic field greens
Spinach
Swiss chard, mustard greens, kale, or other leafy green
    vegetables
Tomatoes
Tomato sauce
Zucchini

Proteins

Boneless, skinless chicken breasts
Eggs
Fish (fresh, when possible, or frozen); choose salmon,
    cod, and tuna if available
Ground chicken or ground turkey (white or dark meat)

Ground sirloin or a lean cut of beef (less than
    5 percent fat)
High-protein bars (8–10 g of protein per bar)
Low-fat cottage cheese
Nonfat yogurt
Skim or soy milk
Soft cheese (Farmer's cheese, blue cheese, fresh
    mozzarella)
Soy protein powder
Tofu
Turkey or chicken breast sandwich meat (nitrate-
    and antibiotic-free)

Complex Carbohydrates

Almonds (unsalted and raw)
Brown rice
Cereal (high protein, high fiber, whole grain, unsweet-
    ened, or low sugar; no granola), like Back to Nature's
    Energy Start, Nature's Path's Optimum Power, and
    Kashi's 7 whole grain nuggets
Kalamata or green olives
Lentils and/or beans (such as great northern beans or
    black-eyed peas), dry or canned
Waffles (frozen spelt or whole grain)
Whole-wheat pasta
Whole-grain or whole-wheat bread, or flat bread
    (like pita) for wraps

Fats

Almond or peanut butter
Extra-virgin olive oil

Sweets

Dried figs
Honey
Pure maple syrup
Raisins
Sugarless fruit spread
Dates

Miscellaneous

Balsamic vinegar
Herbal teas (such as chamomile, mint, lemon, ginger)
Kosher salt
Pepper
Splenda or Stevia (sweeteners)

Cooking Methods

- Grill, bake, or sauté meats and fish in olive oil.
- Steam or grill vegetables, or stir-fry them in a small amount of olive oil.
- To cook fish, sprinkle it with lemon juice on both sides and cover it in a mixture of flour seasoned with lemon pepper, oregano, or dill and salt. Shake off the excess flour and sauté it in olive oil until it's done to your taste.
- Some types of fish like cod and salmon lend themselves just as easily to baking. Simply pat dry the fish, season with lemon-pepper or citrus-pepper, fresh lemon juice, dill, salt, and pepper. Drizzle with olive oil and bake uncovered in an oil-coated baking dish. For a steamed effect, simply wrap the seasoned fish in aluminum foil and bake until tender.

- To prepare meats for grilling, brush them with a mixture of olive oil, lemon juice, citrus or lemon pepper, basil, and oregano. You may also add crushed garlic. For added flavor, drizzle the same mixture over the meat after grilling while it is still hot.
- If you are making grilled sandwiches and don't have a panini grill, use a heavy skillet with a lid instead.

Menu Planning

- Choose three meals and two snacks a day.
- Variety is good for the soul but not for your waistline! Just like your brain thrives and grows when you surround yourself with diverse sensory pleasures, so does your appetite. The eating guidelines included below are designed to keep you healthy even if you choose more or less the same foods every day. You can help your chances of weight loss by eating the same breakfast, lunch, and dinner over a period of a few days.
- Meal and snack choices are listed from the *most* healthful to the *least* healthful. Try to use the first option on each list for breakfast, lunch, and dinner. If that's not possible, try switching between meals; if you chose from the bottom of the list at breakfast, choose the top of the list for dinner regardless of the type of meal, breakfast, lunch, dinner, or snack, if you are still hungry . . . choose the next item(s) on the list. If you are still hungry after eating one option, choose the next on the list.
- If you have one of those days when you can't stop eating, go ahead and overeat breakfast foods.

- Feel free to overeat fruits and vegetables (only those listed here).
- Try to space out your meals and not eat too much at any given sitting. Certainly plan any overeating well before dinner.
- When you crave more food or have a sweet or savory craving, choose *only* among the foods listed from any of the menus.
- If dinner is your main meal, make it a larger portion than lunch by adding more vegetables and hard-cooked egg whites. Reverse if your main meal is lunch.
- Alternate your meat selection. For example, have fish on Monday and Friday, chicken on Sunday and Tuesday, a meatless Wednesday, and lean red meat on Thursday and Saturday.
- Choose one meal from each of the following lists every day.
- A serving of meat is 3 ounces.

Breakfast

- 1 cup of yogurt mixed with 1 scoop of protein powder (preferably soy) and topped with a medley of fresh or frozen berries
- ¾ to 1 cup of high-protein cereal with skim or soy milk and ½–¾ cup of fruit
- 1½ cups of yogurt topped with ¾ cup high-protein cereal and ½–¾ cup of fruit
- A fruit smoothie made with ice, orange juice, a banana, fresh or frozen fruit (such as berries) and 1 scoop of protein powder

- 2 pieces of whole-wheat toast with 1 tablespoon of almond butter or fruit spread
- 3 egg whites (or two whole eggs plus one egg white) scrambled plain or in an omelet with onions, tomatoes, and spinach topped with olives
- 2 hard-boiled eggs (or four hard-boiled egg whites) cut up in chunks; sprinkled with lemon juice, salt, and pepper; and made into a sandwich using 2 slices of whole-grain toast.
- 1 toasted whole-grain English muffin or multigrain bagel with 2 poached eggs drizzled with olive oil, lemon, and pepper

Lunch

- Fresh tomatoes, basil, and soft cheese (fresh mozzarella or any Framer's soft cheese) drizzled with olive oil, oregano, or fresh basil and accompanied by assorted fruit
- Lentil or bean soup; a slice of whole-grain toast topped with cheese or olives; and 2 whole fruits (apples, nectarines, or 1½ cups of melon or a berry medley)
- 1½ to 2 cups of nonfat yogurt mixed with berries or banana slices and 2 scoops of protein powder (You can also warm this up and use it as a dessert.)
- A vegetable medley of steamed or boiled multicolored vegetables, like carrots, zucchini, sweet onion, celery, baby squash, and small potatoes with 2 hard-boiled egg whites and 1 slice of low-fat cheese on whole-grain bread as a side.
- A salad of field greens topped with tomatoes, cucumbers, onions, olives, and a choice of grilled lean meat (chicken or beef), fish, or tofu; drizzled with

balsamic vinegar and olive oil (You can add a hard-boiled egg for extra protein.)

- Turkey, chicken, or fish served with steamed vegetables seasoned with olive oil, oregano, and lemon juice
- A turkey sandwich with field greens and tomatoes on whole-grain bread that has been brushed with a mixture of olive oil, lemon, and oregano; a side serving of fruit
- 2 thin slices of low-fat cheese in 2 slices of whole-grain bread, grilled panini-style; a side salad of mixed beans (Variation: Substitute ⅓ cup of your choice of vegetables—zucchini, onions, tomatoes, fresh basil—for the cheese.)
- A mixture of grilled lean beef or turkey, onion, and tomato drizzled with olive oil and lemon; seasoned with salt, pepper, and oregano or fresh basil; and served as a sandwich or panini on a whole-grain bun
- Grilled lean meat, or grilled eggplant and zucchini, with tzatziki sauce; assorted fruit, plain or drizzled with honey

Dinner

- Field greens, onions, cucumbers, and tomatoes tossed lightly with a balsamic vinegar–olive oil dressing and topped with soy-marinated salmon or 3 ounces of any grilled or baked lean meat
- A bowl of bean or lentil soup, toasted whole-grain bread cubes, tomatoes, olives, and cheese
- 1 cup of blanched or boiled rapini (broccoli rabe) with lemon juice; ½ cup of steamed spring potatoes drizzled with 1 teaspoon of olive oil; 2 soft-boiled eggs

- A 5-ounce grilled or oven-broiled turkey burger on a whole-wheat bun; ⅓ cup mixed-bean salad or field green salad
- A broiled or baked fish filet—salmon, tilapia, halibut, ahi, or red snapper—seasoned with lemon oil, dill, or oregano, and served with a steamed vegetable medley
- Whole-wheat pasta tossed with grilled or steamed asparagus and peas, topped with a few shavings of Parmesan or crumbled farmer's cheese
- Whole-wheat pasta topped with ½ cup marinara sauce, 1 cup diced vegetables, and 1 tablespoon grated low-fat Parmesan cheese
- Mediterranean-style sautéed fish; spinach sautéed with olive oil and garlic
- Grilled fish or chicken; sautéed spinach and garlic
- Meat loaf (made with ground turkey, onions, and red peppers) with steamed or grilled vegetables
- Any lean meat or meat loaf and seasoned field greens rolled in a whole-wheat flat bread wrap; side serving of herbed potato salad made with 1 cup boiled potatoes (diced or sliced in rounds), olive oil, lemon, oregano, scallions, and dill
- 1 cup of spinach sautéed in garlic, olive oil, and lemon juice; ½ cup of brown rice; 5 ounces of lean baked or grilled meat, a meatless burger, or a chicken patty

Desserts

- Orange, or any citrus, sections
- Fat-free vanilla yogurt with sliced apples and cinnamon

- Seasonal fruit, or raisins and dried figs
- Fat-free yogurt topped with fresh fruit or no-sugar-added berry preserves
- Low-fat berry yogurt topped with ¼ cup of cereal
- Yogurt and honey
- Fresh fruit salad topped with chopped nuts, honey, and cinnamon
- Bananas topped with cinnamon or cocoa powder
- A piece of whole-wheat toast topped with honey or maple syrup (Think French toast without the fat.)
- A whole-grain or spelt waffle with syrup (Have this only if you can limit yourself to one waffle; otherwise, choose something else.)
- Berries or cubed apples topped with strawberry non-fat yogurt
- 1 cup of grapes, mango slices, or cubed melon

Snacks

- Sliced yellow and red tomatoes sprinkled with olive oil, balsamic vinegar, and basil
- A cucumber cut lengthwise and yellow and red pepper strips with hummus
- A piece of whole-grain toast plain or topped with sliced tomatoes
- Three hard-boiled eggs (discard two yolks) with 1 teaspoon of olive oil and lemon juice on a slice of whole-grain toast
- A handful of almonds or pecans (highly caloric)
- Field greens or baby spinach with hard-boiled eggs and olives (optional), tossed with balsamic vinegar and olive oil

- Tomato and soft-cheese slices topped with fresh basil and sprinkled with olive oil
- Kalamata olives with a slice of whole-grain toast
- Whole-wheat or spelt pita crackers with lemon or roasted pepper hummus
- 1 or 2 soft-boiled eggs (or egg whites) with a whole-grain cracker and 1 piece of fresh apple, pear, banana, orange, peach, or nectarine
- 1 or 2 slices of lean deli meat such as turkey or turkey ham.

Conclusion

Brains are in vogue! After decades of looking to outside sources like medications, diets, and surgery for solutions and treatments for weight management, the focus is now shifting inward; we're looking to the body and the brain to understand why we do the things we do, especially when our actions have consistently harmful consequences.

Following this trend, you have just learned to apply advances in neuroscience to benefit your body and your weight goals. For example, you have learned to harness your brain's braking power to allow you to pause and think before you act on a craving, and simple techniques to shift brain activity away from your emotional brain that leads to bottom-up eating to reflective areas that help you consider consequences and top-down healthy eating.

Internal Strategies for Weight Management

The following are the key elements to take with you from this book.

- **Develop brain fitness before dieting.** Self-defeating behaviors like unhealthy eating are habitual and deeply rooted. To break free of these patterns, you need to get in shape. You wouldn't run a marathon without proper training. Why expect to breeze through the challenges of weight management without first conditioning your brain? It will serve as your legs and lungs to carry you comfortably through the lengthy weight-loss process. Regardless of the diet method you choose to lose weight, begin with a fitness program for your brain.

- **If you have trained your eating brain once, you can do it again.** You have absolute proof that you are capable of training your brain, albeit not in the direction you intended. You have inadvertently taught it to rely on the feel-good chemicals that are released when you eat high-calorie foods. You can now retrain it to help break that cycle.

- **You become what you eat.** Healthy foods lessen your cravings because they interact with your brain and the rest of your body to produce an experience of purpose, meaning, satisfaction, and calm awareness. Unhealthy foods also interact with your body and turn on genes and chemicals that distort your body's function and balance.

- **Excess weight hurts your mind.** You know that obesity destroys your health, but remember that a learning brain is a healthy brain. A healthy mind with the ability to distinguish motives, identify patterns and see forthcoming trends, problem solve, and focus is a vital commodity and arguably all you need to succeed in life. The foods that you find so delicious harm your brain's cognitive skills and take away clarity of intellect, learning, thinking, and reasoning.

• **Food is the new status symbol.** You can usually predict a person's socioeconomic status just by a quick glance at their grocery cart or pantry. Think of junk food and high-fat, high-calorie foods as low quality. You deserve better. Healthier food is at the top of the scale—high in protein, fresh fruits, and vegetables; low in fatty animal products and synthetic foods.

You may not be a millionaire rocket scientist, but when you fill your food basket with the foods included in the BrainMed Diet, you will certainly be eating like one.

• **Learn to judge size accurately.** In a society with an overweight majority, it's hard to know whether you are overweight or average just by comparing yourself to others. It's best not to rely on other people's comments ("You look fine. You don't need to lose weight. You're too skinny.") as a basis for judging your weight; rather use your body mass index or scale weight. Remember that others will tend to evaluate your size based on their own.

• **Modify internal cravings.** You don't have to follow your brain's persistent calls for food deliveries. Your brain is only looking for a dopamine or serotonin high, which in your case may mean eating pleasure; keep in mind that any pleasure will do to satisfy the brain's quest for pleasure.

• **A happy brain is a satisfied brain.** Remember that your brain thrives when you spend every day surrounded by healthy challenges on one hand and a rich, beautiful environment on the other. Barring illness, disasters, and death, imagine your day as a pie chart divided into two parts: you spend perhaps 60 percent of your time in kind interaction with others and the world around you in an enriching environment and the other 40 percent being challenged and productive. You can work the ratios to suit your needs.

You know by now that unplanned or impulsive eating done on autopilot when you are neither hungry nor satisfied is a major reason for excess weight. Implementing the OPT tools helps you boost awareness and control your needs so you can be in a better position to apply healthy alternatives to self-destructive eating. There are many methods for retraining your brain aside from OPT, key among them are yoga, meditation, psychotherapy, some medications, and neurofeedback (an effective technique that helps fine-tune the brain's electrical brainwaves toward healthier patterns). Each of these methods has the potential to boost your ability for self-regulation and weight loss, but combining two or more can speed up the process for faster results. They all have a common goal: to help reroute and reconfigure the brain away from self-defeating "ruts" to new, more adaptive patterns. Each of these methods aims to give you the ability to regulate your weight internally by helping smooth out your brain. Use the resources at the end of this book, as well as those provided in your community, to jump-start your progress. The momentum from OPT can help you move forward with weight loss because it makes lifestyle changes easier.

I wish you luck; success; and a happy, flourishing brain.

Resources

The following list of useful references and links can be used to widen your grasp of how dynamic approaches are used to promote and preserve wellness. Combining neurofeedback with OPT when possible, is highly recommended.

Body Mass Index Calculation

To get your body mass index (BMI), calculate your height in inches and square that number. Divide your weight in pounds by the squared number, then multiply the result by 703. According to the Centers for Disease Control and Prevention (CDC), a BMI of at least 30 indicates obesity (someone who is 5 foot, 4 inches would have to weigh 175 pounds); someone who has a BMI of 25 is defined as overweight. For more information, refer to the CDC's website at cdc.gov/nccdphp/dnpa/bmi/calc-bmi.htm.

Neurofeedback

The following sites can provide more information on neurofeedback and help you locate providers in your area:

Applied Psychophysiology and Biofeedback (aapb.org/
i4a/pages/index.cfm?pageid=1)
International Society for Neuronal Regulation (http://
isnr.org)

Books on Nonlinear Weight-Loss Plans

Hyman, M. *Ultrametabolism: The Simple Plan for Automatic
Weight Loss.* New York: Scribner, 2006.
Roisen, M, and M. Oz. *You on a Diet: The Owners Manual for
Waist Management.* New York: Free Press, 2006.

Books on General Approaches to Brain Fitness

Chernov, F. B. *The Sharper Mind.* New York: Prentice Hall,
1997.
Restak, R. *The New Brain: How the Modern Age Is Rewiring
Our Mind.* New York: Rodale, 2003.
Siegel, J. S. *The Mindful Brain. Reflection and Attunement in
the Cultivation of Well-Being.* New York: W. W. Norton
& Company, 2007.
Zaldy, T. *Age-Proof Your Mind: Detect, Delay, and Prevent
Memory Loss—Before It's Too Late.* New York: Warner
Books, 2005.

References

Introduction

Cajal, S. R. *Estudios Sobre la Degeneración y Regeneración del Sistema Nervioso*. Madrid: Moya. 1913–1914. [Degeneration and Regeneration of the Nervous System]. Translated and edited by Raoul M. May. London: Oxford University Press, 1928.

Friedman, J. M. "Obesity in the New Millennium." *Nature* 604, no. 6778 (2000): 632–34.

Lisle, D. J. and A. Goldhamer. *The Pleasure Trap: Mastering the Hidden Force that Undermines Health and Happiness*. Summertown, Tenn.: Healthy Living Publications, 2003.

Midgley, M. *Beast and Man: The Roots of Human Nature*. London: Routledge, 1995.

Wansink, B. "Environmental Factors that Increase the Food Intake and Consumption Volume of Unknowing Consumers." *Annual Review of Nutrition* 24 (2004): 455–79.

Chapter 1

Baumeister, R. "Binge Eating: Vanishing Bite by Bite." In *Escaping the Self: Alcoholism, Spirituality Masochism, and Other Flights from Burden of Selfhood*. New York: Basic Books, 1991.

Carter, R. "The Emerging Landscape." Chapter 1 in *Mapping the Mind*. Berkeley, Calif.: University of California Press, 1999.

Fierro, M. P. "The Obesity Epidemic: How States Can Trim the 'Fat.'" *North Carolina Medical Journal* 63, no. 6 (2002): 304. *World Health Organization Report on Obesity*. 1997.

Friedman, J. M. "Obesity in the New Millennium." *Nature* 604, no. 6778 (2000): 632–34.

Hsu, L. K. "Can Dieting Cause an Eating Disorder?" *Psychological Medicine* 27, no. 3 (1997): 509–13.

Joseph, R. *The Naked Neuron*. New York: Plenum Press, 1993.

LeDoux, J. *The Emotional Brain*. New York: Simon and Schuster, 1996.

Norman, D. *Emotional Design: Why We Love (or Hate) Everyday Things*. New York: Basic Books, 2004.

Perez-Tilve, D., J. Stern, and M. Tschöp. "The Brain and the Metabolic Syndrome: Not a Wireless Connection." *Endocrinology* 147, no. 3 (2006): 1136–39.

Pinker, S. "A Biological Understanding of Human Nature." In *The New Humanists: Science at the Edge*. Edited by John Brockman. New York. Barnes and Noble Books, 2003.

Polivy, J. "Psychological Consequences of Food Restriction." *Journal of the American Dietetic Association* 96, no. 6 (1996): 589–92.

Seeley, R. J. and D. A. York. "Fuel Sensing and the Central Nervous System (CNS): Implications for the Regulation of Energy Balance and the Treatment for Obesity." *Obesity Review* 6, no. 3 (2005): 259–65.

Stanley, S., K. Wynne, B. McGowan, and S. Bloom. "Hormonal Regulation of Food Intake." *Physiological Review* 85, no. 4 (2005): 1131–158.

Wansink, B. "Environmental Factors that Increase the Food Intake and Consumption Volume of Unknowing Consumers." *Annual Review of Nutrition* 24 (2004): 455–79.

Williams, G., J. A. Harrold, and D. J. Cutler. "The Hypothalamus and the Regulation of Energy Homeostasis: Lifting the Lid on a Black Box." *Proceedings of the Nutritional Society* 59, no. 3 (2000): 385–96.

Wrangham, R. "The Evolution of Cooking." In *The New Humanists: Science at the Edge.* Edited by John Brockman. New York: Barnes and Noble Books, 2003.

Chapter 2

Amen, D. G. *Change Your Brain, Change Your Life.* New York: Three Rivers Press, 1998.

Blum, K. "Reward Deficiency Syndrome." *American Scientist* 84 (1996): 132–45.

Cappuccio, F. "Sleep Deprivation Doubles Risks of Obesity in Both Children and Adults." *Science Daily,* July 13, 2006, sciencedaily.com.

Carter, R. "Beneath the Surface." Chapter 3 in *Mapping the Mind.* Berkeley, Calif.: University of California Press, 1999.

De Parigi, A., J. F. Gautier, K. Chen, et al. "Mapping the Brain Responses to Hunger and Satiation Using Positron Emission Tomography." *Annals of the New York Academy of Sciences* 967 (2002): 389–97.

Dosenbach, N., K. Visscher, E. Palmer, et al. "A Core System for the Implementation of Task Sets." *Neuron* 50, no. 5 (2006): 799–812.

Dum, J. J., et al. "Densely Caloric Foods Stimulate the Opiod System Inside the Hypothalamus." *Pharmacology Biochemistry and Behavior* 18 (1983).

Emory University Hospital's Brighthouse Institute for Thought Sciences, "The Brighthouse Institute for Thought Sciences Claims It's Closing the Gap Between Business and Science," news release, June 22, 2002.

Friedman, J. M. "Fat in All the Wrong Places." *Nature* 415, no. 6778 (2000): 268–69.

Gautier, J. F., K. Chen, A. D. Salbe, et al. "Differential Brain Responses to Satiation in Obese and Lean Men." *Diabetes* 49, no. 5 (2001): 838–46.

Hotz, R. L. "Mine Visions of Sugar Plums Danced in His Head." *Los Angeles Times*, February 27, 2005.

Hyman, M. *Nutrigenomics: How Food 'Talks' to Your Genes to Turn on Messages of Health or Disease.* drhyman.com/nutrigenomics.php.

Johnson, C., C. Lewis, and J. Hagan. "The Syndrome of Bulimia: Review and Synthesis." *Psychiatric Clinics of North America* 7 (1984): 247–73.

Johnson, D. K., C. H. Wilkins, and J. C. Morris. "Accelerated Weight Loss in Alzheimer's Disease Precedes Diagnosis." *Archives of Neurology* 63 (2006): 1312–317.

Kaput, J. "Decoding the Pyramid: A Systems-Biological Approach to Nutrigenomics." *Annals of the New York Academy of Science* 1055 (2005): 64–79.

Kuehn, B. "Brain Scans: Genes Provide Addiction Clues." *JAMA* 297, no. 13 (2007): 1419–421.

Lisle, D. J. and A. Goldhamer. *The Pleasure Trap: Mastering the Hidden Force that Undermines Health and Happi-*

ness. Summertown, Tenn.: Healthy Living Publications, 2003.

Maguire, E., R. S. J. Frackowiak, C. D. Frith, et al. "Recalling Routes Around London: Activation of the Right Hippocampus in Taxi Drivers." *Journal of Neuroscience* 17 (1997): 7103–110.

Ng, D. and R. W. Jeffery. "Relationship Between Perceived Stress and Health Behavior in a Sample of Working Adults." *Health Psychology* 22, no. 6 (2005): 638–42.

Olsson, A., E. Phelps, and K. Nearing. "Learning Fears by Observing Others: The Neural Systems of Social Fear Transmission." *Social Cognitive and Affective Neuroscience,* March 2007, sciencedaily.com.

Rothenberger, A., B. Blanz, G. Lehmkuhl, et al. "What Happens to Electrical Brain Activity When Anorectic Females Gain Weight?" *European Archives of Psychiatry and Clinical Neurosurgery* 240, no. 3 (1991): 144–47.

Schwartz, J. and C. Byrd-Bredbenner. "Portion Distortion: Typical Portion Sizes Selected by Young Adults." *Journal of the American Dietetic Association* 106, no. 9 (2006): 1412–418.

Seeley, R. J. and D. York. "Fuel Sensing and the Central Nervous System (CNS): Implications for the Regulation of Energy Balance and the Treatment for Obesity." *Obesity Reviews* 6, no. 3 (2005): 259–65.

Small, G. *The Longevity Bible: 8 Essential Strategies for Keeping Your Mind Sharp and Your Body Young.* New York: Hyperion, 2006.

Steinbaum, E. and N. Miller. "Obesity from Eating Elicited by Daily Stimulation of Hypothalamus." *American Journal of Physiology* 208 (1965): 1–5.

Thayer, R. *Calm Energy: How People Regulate Mood with Food and Exercise.* London: Oxford University Press, 2003.

Tremblay, A. "Children Who Sleep Less Are Three Times More Likely to Be Overweight." *International Journal of Obesity*, March 29, 2006, sciencedaily.com.

Van Cauter, E. "Sleep Loss Boosts Appetite, May Encourage Weight Gain." *Annals of Internal Medicine*, December 7, 2004, sciencedaily.com.

Wang, G. J. and N. Volkow. "How Can Drug Addiction Help Us Understand Obesity?" *Nature Neuroscience* 8, no. 5 (2005): 555–60.

Weltzin, T. E. and W. H. Kaye. "Serotonin Activity in Anorexia and Bulimia Nervosa: Relationship to the Modulation of Feeding and Mood." *Journal of Clinical Psychiatry* 52 (1991): 41–48.

Wynne, S. S., B. McGowan, and S. Bloom. "Hormonal Regulation of Food Intake." *Physiology Review* 85, no. 4 (2005): 1131–158.

Yoon, C., A. Gutchess, F. Feinberg, and T. Polk. "A Functional Magnetic Resonance Imaging Study of Neural Dissociations Between Brand and Person Judgments." *Journal of Consumer Research* 33 (2006): 31–40.

Chapter 3

Amen, D. G. *Change Your Brain, Change Your Life*. New York: Three Rivers Press, 1998.

Carter, R. "Beneath the Surface." Chapter 3 in *Mapping the Mind*. Berkeley, Calif.: University of California Press, 1998.

———. "Higher Ground." Chapter 8 in *Mapping the Mind*. Berkeley, Calif.: University of California Press, 1998.

Herman, C. P. and D. Mack. "Restrained and Unrestrained Eating." *Journal of Personality* 43, no. 4 (1975): 647–60.

Horvath, T. and G. Xiao-Bing. "Input Organization and Plasticity of Hypocretin Neurons: Possible Clues to Obesity's Association with Insomnia." *Cell Metabolism* 1, no. 4 (2005): 279–86.

Jia-Hong, G. "Effect of Satiation on Brain Activity in Obese and Lean Women." *Obesity Research* 9 (2001): 729–30.

Mills, J. K. and G. D. Andrianopoulos. "The Relationship Between Childhood Onset Obesity and Psychopathology in Adulthood." *Journal of Psychology* 127, no. 5 (1993): 547–51.

Waedle, J. "Eating Style: A Validation Study of the Dutch Eating Behaviour Questionnaire in Normal Subjects and Women with Eating Disorders." *Journal of Psychosomatic Research* 31, no. 2 (1987): 161–69.

Chapter 4

Andrianopoulos G. D., R. L. Nelson, C. T. Bombeck, and G. Souza. "The Role of Physical Activity on 1,2-dimethylhydrazine Rat Colon Carcinogenesis." *Anticancer Research* 7, no. 5 (1987): 849–52.

Andrianopoulos G. D., R. L. Nelson, C. T. Bombeck, G. Souza, and L. M. Nyhus. "The Protective Influence of Physical Activity on Carcinogenesis in the Rat Colorectum." *The Physiologist* 30, no. 4 (1987): 134.

Avanzini, G., L. Lopez, S. Koelsch, et al. eds. 2006. Annals of the New York Academy of Sciences. *The Neurosciences and Music II: From Perception to Performance*. Vol. 1060.

Aziz-Zadeh, L., S. Wilson, G. Rizzolatti, and M. Iacoboni. "A Comparison of Premotor Areas Activated by Action

Observation and Action Phrases." *Current Biology* 16, no. 18 (2006): 1818–823.

Bennett, E., M. Diamond, D. Krech, and M. Rosenzweig. "Chemical and Anatomical Plasticity of Brain." *Science* 146 (1964): 610–19.

Björklund, A. and O. Lindvall. "Self-Repair in the Brain." *Neurobiology: Nature* 405 (2000): 892–95.

Black, J. E., A. M. Sirevaag, C. S. Wallace, M. H. Savin, and W. T. Greenough. "Effects of Complex Experience on Somatic Growth and Organ Development in Rats." *Developmental Psychobiology* 22 (1989): 727–52.

Brownlee, C. "Buff and Brainy," *Science News* 169, no. 8 (2006): 122. sciencenews.org/articles/20060225/bob10.asp.

Dallman, M., N. Pecoraro, S. Akana, et al. "Chronic Stress and Obesity: A New View of 'Comfort Food.'" *Neuroscience*. Proceedings of the National Academy of Sciences USA, September 15, 2003, pnas.org/cgi/content/abstract/1934666100v1.

Evans G. W., P. Kim, A. H. Ting, et al. "Cumulative Risk, Maternal Responsiveness and Allostatic Load Among Young Adolescents." *Developmental Psychology* 43 (2007): 341–51.

Gazzola, V., L. Aziz-Zadeh, and C. Keysers. "Empathy and the Somatotopic Mirror System in Humans." *Current Biology* 16, no. 18 (2006): 1824–829.

Gould, E., A. Beylin, P. Tanapat, et al. "Learning Enhances Adult Neurogenesis in the Hippocampal Formation." *Nature Neuroscience* 2 (1999): 260–65.

Gould, E., A. J. Reeves, M. S. A. Graziano, and C. G. Gross. "Neurogenesis in the Neocortex of Adult Primates." *Science* 286 (1999): 548–52.

Gould, E. "The Reinvention of Self: A Mind-Altering Idea Reveals How Life Affects the Brain." *Seed Magazine* 60 (2006).

Gustufson D. R., E. Rothenberg, K. Blennow, et al. "An 18 Year Follow-Up of Overweight and Risk for Alzheimer's Disease." *Archives of Internal Medicine* 203, no. 163 (2005): 1524–528.

Horvath, T., and G. Xiao-Bing. "Input Organization and Plasticity of Hypocretin Neurons: Possible Clues to Obesity's Association with Insomnia." *Cell Metabolism* 1, no. 4 (2005): 279–86.

Kantrowitz, B. "The Quest for Rest." *Newsweek*, May 8, 2006, news.uchicago.edu/citations/06/060429.cauter-nw.html.

Kempermann, G., H. G. Kuhn, and F. H. Gage. "More Hippocampal Neurons in Adult Mice Living in an Enriched Environment." *Nature* 386, no. 6624 (1997): 493–95.

Kramer A. F., S. Hahn, N. J. Cohen, et al. "Ageing, Fitness, and Neurocognitive Function." *Nature* 400 (1999): 418–19.

Lehrer, J. "The Reinvention of the Self." *Seed Magazine* 58 (2006).

Mirescu C., J. D. Peters, and E. Gould. "Early Life Experiences Alters Response of Adult Neurogenesis to Stress." *National Neuroscience* 7 (2004): 841–46.

Mirescu C., J. D. Peters, L. Noiman, and E. Gould. "Sleep Deprivation Inhibits Adult Neurogenesis in the Hippocampus by Elevating Glucocorticoids." *Proceedings of the National Academy of Science USA* 103 (2006): 19170–9175.

North, A. C., D. J. Hargreaves, J. McKendrick, et al. "In Store Music Affects Product Choice." *Nature* 390, no. 6656 (1997): 132.

Small, G. *The Longevity Bible: 8 Essential Strategies for Keeping Your Mind Sharp and Your Body Young.* New York: Hyperion, 2006.

Trakas, K. "Study Shows Obesity Bad for the Mind, Too." *Science Daily,* sciencedaily.com/releases/2001/05/010529071515.htm.

Van Cauter, E. "Sleep Loss Boosts Appetite, May Encourage Weight Gain." December 6, 2004, uchospitals.edu/news/2004/20041206-sleep.html.

Van Cauter, E., K. Knutson, R. Leproult, K. Spiegel, et al. "The Impact of Sleep Deprivation on Hormones and Metabolism." *Medscape Neurology and Neurosurgery* 7, no. 1 (2005). medscape.com/viewarticle/502825.

Wansink, B. "Popcorn Lovers Eat More When Given Bigger Containers, Test Shows," news release, University of Illinois at Urbana Champaign, March 5, 1999.

Chapter 5

Chartrand, T. L., and J. A. Bargh. "The Chameleon Effect: The Perception–Behavior Link of Social Interaction." *Journal of Personality and Social Psychology* 76, no. 6 (1999): 893–910.

Christakis, N. A. and J. H. Fowler. "The Spread of Obesity in a Large Social Network Over 32 years." *New England Journal Medicine* 357 (2007): 370–79.

Davidson, R. J., J. Kabat-Zinn, J. Schumacher, et al. "Alterations in Brain and Immune Function Produced by Mindfulness Meditation." *Psychosomatic Medicine* 65 (2003): 564–70.

Kosslyn, S. "What Shape Are a German Shepherd's Ears?" In *The New Humanists: Science At the Edge.* Edited by John Brockman. New York: Barnes and Noble Books, 2003.

Luciana, M., H. M. Conklin, C. J. Hooper, and R. S. Yarger. "The Development of Nonverbal Working Memory and Executive Control Processes in Adolescents." *Child Development* 76, no. 3 (2005): 697–712.

Moran, T. H. and S. Gad. "Looking for Love in All the Wrong Places?" *Cell Metabolism* 3, no. 4 (2006): 233–34.

Norman, D. A. *Emotional Design: Why We Love (or Hate) Everyday Things.* New York: Basic Books, 2004.

Perez, C. "The Benefits of Aromatherapy: M. D. Anderson Teaches How to Soothe and Heal." www.medicalnews today.com/medicalnews.php?newsid=50591.

Ramachandran V. S. "Mirror Neurons and Imitation Learning as the Driving Force Behind the Great Leap Forward in Human Evolution." http://edge .org/3rd_culture/ramachandran/ramachandran_p1.

Ranganathan, V. K., V. Siemionow, J. Z. Liu, et al. "From Mental Power to Muscle Power: Gaining Strength by Using Your Mind." *Neuropsychologia* 42 (2004): 944–56.

Riskind, J. H., W. S. Rholes, J. Eggers. "The Velten Mood Induction Procedure: Effects on Mood and Memory." *Journal of Consulting and Clinical Psychology* 50, no. 1 (1982): 146–47.

Rizzolatti G. "Mirror Neuron System." *Annual Review Neuroscience* 27 (2004): 169–92.

Rizzolatti G., L. Fogassi, and V. Gallese. "Neurophysilogical Mechanisms Underlying the Understanding and Imitation of Action." *Nature Review Neuroscience* 2 (2001): 661–70.

Rosmond, R. "Obesity and Cortisol." *Nutrition* 16, no. 10 (2000): 924–36.

Strattford, T. and M. Webb. *Mind Hacks: Tips and Tools for Using Your Brain.* Sebastopol, Calif.: O'Reilly, 2005.

Timmerman, G. "Restaurant Eating in Nonpurge Binge-Eating Women." *Western Journal of Nursing Research* 28 (2006): 811–24.

Velten, E. "A Laboratory Task for Induction of Mood States." *Behavior Research and Therapy* 6 (1968): 473–82.

Wansink, B. "Popcorn Lovers Eat More When Given Bigger Containers, Test Shows," news release, University of Illinois at Urbana Champaign, March 5, 1999.

Chapter 6

Bobroff, E. and H. Kissileff. "Effects of Changes in Palatability of Food Intake and the Cumulative Food Intake Curve in Man." *Appetite* 7, no. 1 (1986): 85–96.

Clancy, B. "Self Regulation Related to Academic Ability Over and Above Intelligence." *Journal of Child Development* 78, no. 2 (2007): 647–63.

Geier, A. B. and P. Rozin. "Penn Psychologists Believe 'Unit Bias' Determines the Acceptable Amount to Eat," http://www.upen.edu/researchatpenn/article.php?999&hlt.

Hsee, C. K., Y. Rottenstreich, and X. Zhixing. "When Is Better? On the Relationship Between Magnitude and Subjective Value." *Current Directions in Psychological Science* 14, no. 5 (2005): 234–37.

Timmerman, G. "Restaurant Eating in Nonpurge Binge-Eating Women," *Western Journal Nursing Research* 28 (2006): 811–24.

Treit, D., M. L. Spetch, and J. A. Deutsch. "Variety in the Flavor of Food Enhances Eating in the Rat: A Controlled Demonstration." *Physiology and Behavior* 30, no. 2 (1983): 207–11.

Wansink, B. *Mindless Eating: Why We Eat More Than We Think.* New York: Bantam Dell, 2006.

Wansink, B., J. Painter, and J. North. "Bottomless Bowls: Why Visual Cues of Portion Size May Influence Intake." *Obesity Research* 13, no. 1 (2005): 93–100.

Chapter 7

Battino, M. and M. S. Ferreiro. "Ageing and the Mediterranean Diet: A Review of the Role of Dietary Fats." *Public Health Nutrition* 7 (2004): 953–58.

Braverman, E. *The Edge Effect: Reverse or Prevent Alzheimers, Aging, Memory Loss, Weight Gain, Sexual Dysfunction and More.* New York: Sterling Publishing Co., 2004.

Kalogeropoulos, N., A. Chiou, A. Mylona, et al. "Recovery and Distribution of Natural Antioxidants (α-Tocopherol, Polyphenols, and Terpenic Acids) After Pan-Frying of Mediterranean Finfish in Virgin Olive Oil." *Food Chemistry* 100, no. 2 (2007): 509–17.

Mattson, M. P., S. Chan, and W. Duan. "Modification of Brain Aging and Neurodegenerative Disorders by Gene, Diet, and Behavior." *Physiological Reviews* 82, no. 3 (2002): 637–72.

Morris, M. C. "Vegetable Consumption Slows Rate of Cognitive Decline." *Neurology* 67 (2006): 1370–376.

Persky, V. and G. D. Andrianopoulos. "Etiology of Colon Cancer: Is It All in the Diet?" In *Problems in General Surgery: Controversies of Colon Cancer.* Edited by R. L. Nelson. 4, no. 1 (1987): 11–23.

Rogers, P. "Healthy Body and Healthy Mind: Long-Term Impact of Diet on Mood and Cognitive Function." *Proceedings of the Nutrition Society* 60 (2001): 135–43.

Sohal, R. and R. W. Richard. "Oxidative Stress, Caloric Restriction, and Aging." *Science* 273, no. 5271 (1996): 59–63.

Stavric, B. "Role of Chemopreventers in Human Diet." *Clinical Biochemistry* 27, no. 5 (1994): 319–32.

Van Duyn, M. A., and E. Pivonka. "Overview of the Health Benefits of Fruit and Vegetable Consumption for the Dietetics Professional." *Journal of the American Dietetic Association* 100, no. 12 (2000): 1511–1521.

Velten E. A Laboratory Task for Induction of Mood States. *Behavioral Research and Therapy* 6 (1968): 473–82.

Wansink, B., J. E. Painter, and J. North. "Bottomless Bowls: Why Visual Cues of Portion Size *May* Influence Food Intake." *Obesity Research* 13 (2005): 93–100.

Index

About the Author

Georgia Andrianopoulos is a physiologic psychologist. She completed her graduate work at Case Western Reserve University in Cleveland and has worked in the field of eating disorders for the past twenty years, first as director of the eating disorders clinic at the University of Illinois Medical Center at Chicago and later in private practice. She has been interviewed by the *Chicago Tribune* and by local radio and television affiliates of NBC and CBS on various aspects of obesity. She has also been interviewed by the Associated Press and has contributed to radio and television segments on obesity and food cravings.

Georgia is the author of numerous original research publications and has contributed chapters for academic books. To learn more about her and her publications and programs, go to www.brainfitnessinc.com.